It's A Matter Of Faith And Life
Volume 3

A Catechism Companion

The Ten Commandments

David M. Albertin

CSS Publishing Company, Inc., Lima, Ohio

IT'S A MATTER OF FAITH AND LIFE — VOLUME 3

Copyright © 1997 by
CSS Publishing Company, Inc.
Lima, Ohio

All rights reserved. No part of this publication may be reproduced in any manner whatsoever without the prior permission of the publisher, except in the case of brief quotations embodied in critical articles and reviews. Inquiries should be addressed to: Permissions, CSS Publishing Company, Inc., P.O. Box 4503, Lima, Ohio 45802-4503.

Scripture quotations are from the *Revised Standard Version of the Bible*, copyrighted 1946, 1952 ©, 1971, 1973, by the Division of Christian Education of the National Council of the Churches of Christ in the USA. Used by permission.

Some scripture quotations are from the *Holy Bible, New International Version*. Copyright © 1973, 1978, 1984 International Bible Society. Used by permission of Zondervan Bible Publishers. All rights reserved.

From Luther's *Small Catechism*, 1986, Copyright 1986 Concordia Publishing House. Used with permission.

Excerpt from *Life Together* by Dietrich Bonhoeffer. English translation copyright © 1954 by Harper & Brothers, copyright renewed 1982 by Helen S. Doberstein. Reprinted by permission of HarperCollins Publishers, Inc.

Library of Congress Cataloging-in-Publication Data

Albertin, David M., 1939-
   It's a matter of faith and life / David M. Albertin.
     p. cm.
    Contents: 1. 1. Baptism, confession, absolution, the office of the keys, and holy communion — v. 2. The Apostles' creed and the Lord's prayer — v. 3. The Ten commandments.
    ISBN 0-7880-0356-9 (pbk. : v. 1). — ISBN 0-7880-0357-7 (pbk. : v. 2). — ISBN 0-7880-0358-5 (pbk. : v. 3)
   1. Luther, Martin, 1483-1546. Kleine Katechismus. 2. Lutheran Church—Catechisms—English. I. Title.
BX8070.L8A7   1997
238'.41—dc21   96-47408
                                                                                                                    CIP

To my three children
Timothy
Jonathan
Kristen
and their children

Table Of Contents

Preface — 7

The Ten Commandments: — 11
The First Commandment

The Ten Commandments: — 19
The Second Commandment

The Ten Commandments: — 27
The Third Commandment

The Ten Commandments: — 33
The Fourth Commandment

The Ten Commandments: — 41
The Fifth Commandment

The Ten Commandments: — 47
The Sixth Commandment

The Ten Commandments: — 53
The Seventh Commandment

The Ten Commandments: — 61
The Eighth Commandment

The Ten Commandments: — 69
The Ninth And Tenth Commandments

The Ten Commandments: — 75
The Conclusion To The Commandments

Preface

It's A Matter Of Faith And Life originally appeared in the form of a script for a television program *(The Lutheran Lexicon)* which appeared on the Michigan City, Indiana, ecumenical community access cable channel. It also has been employed in the catechetical instruction of junior high youth at Immanuel Lutheran Church of Michigan City.

In its present form *It's A Matter Of Faith And Life* appears as a narrative companion to Dr. Martin Luther's *Small Catechism*. It is written in a style that should be attractive to readers of all ages.

Each chapter of *It's A Matter Of Faith And Life* focuses on a part of the *Small Catechism*. For example, there is a chapter on Baptism Part One, the Second Article of the Apostles' Creed, the Third Commandment, the Fourth Petition of the Lord's Prayer, and so forth. Each of these chapters does not exhaust the content of what the Catechism has to say. Rather the chapters focus on a key and significant issue that underlies the particular part being discussed.

It's A Matter Of Faith And Life, this book of words about words which ultimately focuses on the Word, can be employed as a devotional reader or as a supplement to the Catechism in catechetical instruction. The biblical quotes have been taken from the Revised Standard Version of the Bible. Some of them, however, are my own liberal translations and summaries. The references to the *Small Catechism* have been taken from the 1986 edition of *Luther's Small Catechism With Explanation,* Concordia Publishing House, St. Louis, Missouri.

The material in *It's A Matter Of Faith And Life* reflects my five decades of being a Christian. These pages began to be formed by the influence of my parents and the church which I attended as a child. The many references and examples cited have been gleaned from my childhood experiences, the Christian instructors at whose feet I have sat, my own reading and studying, and from what I have encountered as an adult and a pastor. Therefore, precise documentation and citing of sources is frequently absent. Instead, I would like to thank all of those who have had an effect on my Christian formation: my parents, my Sunday School teachers, my various instructors at the three Concordias I attended, and my friends both on the "street" and of the academic.

In other words, this is a book about life, the life of a Christian, and how the six chief parts of the Christian faith as presented in the *Small Catechism* of Dr. Martin Luther interacted with his life and gave shape and direction to it.

God be thanked for the numerous and wonderful ways He has provided for my Christian pilgrimage and growing in the faith. These pages have been written to share with you some of that which has been shared with me.

Soli Deo Gloria

David Albertin
Michigan City, Indiana
Winter 1996

The Ten Commandments

The Ten Commandments:
The First Commandment

❖ ❖ ❖ ❖ ❖

Everybody seems to have a need for some kind of god — for example, a need for a supreme being, a need for ultimate purpose in life, and so forth. Can you add any other reasons why people seem to have a need for some kind of god? Take any one of those reasons and argue both for and against it.

Some people say that even atheists (people who say that they don't believe that there is a god) must constantly say that there is no god, because their consciences will not let them rest. Therefore, they are always trying to convince themselves that there is no god, because they too find it hard to believe that there is no god. What do you think about that?

❖ ❖ ❖ ❖ ❖

Who is God?

It is next to impossible to get unanimous agreement in an answer to that question. But there is little disagreement when it comes to simply asserting that there is a god. However, just any old god will not do. We want to know who is the right one. It is important for us to know who is the right one.

We know that it is important, because the First Commandment says so. It says, "You shall have no other gods" than the right One. Actually God, the right One, says so in that commandment.

God gave the Ten Commandments to Moses at Mount Sinai. Find Mount Sinai on a map. Some people say that the Ten Commandments were to the Hebrew people like the Constitution (and Bill of Rights) is to the American citizen. Both speak of some basic principle by which the people are to live. Both came into being at the time of the birth of a nation. What are some of the other similarities between the birth of these two nations? The Hebrew story can be found in Exodus 1-15.

And so we come now to the Ten Commandments. Next to the cross the Ten Commandments are the most well-known characteristic of the Christian faith. In fact, some people might even think that the Ten Commandments are the most important characteristic of the Christian faith. Perhaps that is so because The Faith is often looked upon as being a system of rules, laws, and commandments by which the faithful are to live. It is often thought that the quality of one's faith is to be judged in terms of how well one keeps the commandments. No wonder, then, that some people think that the most important reason for sending children to Sunday School is so that they can learn the Ten Commandments. Sunday School is supposed to make good little boys and girls out of them. I, however, tell the Sunday School teachers of the church where I serve as pastor that if that is what they think Sunday School is all about, they should resign as teachers — immediately. I don't want the Sunday School teachers of our congregation teaching children that the most important thing about the Christian faith is a system of rules to be obeyed.

Martin Luther compared the use of the Ten Commandments to both a curb (they keep us out of trouble) and a mirror (they reflect our behavior). What are some other images that you can think of which reflect the use of the Commandments? For example, what do the Commandments do? What is the most important function of the Commandments?

That does not mean that the Ten Commandments are not important. They are very important to the living of the Christian life. Martin Luther, for example, said that they are like a curb that keeps us in bounds; they keep us from going over the edge like guard rails along a mountain highway. I like to compare them to one of those bobsled chutes that we see at the time of the Winter Olympics. A team of athletes gets on one of those sleds, and then it hurtles down the chute. It ricochets from one side to the other, but the chute is banked in such a way that the sled will not go flying off of the course. The Commandments are something like that bobsled slide. They are intended to keep us on the track and out of too much trouble.

Even more important, Luther tells us, is that the Commandments are like a mirror. As we look at ourselves reflected in them, we see a reflection of our lives, of how we have lived. These Commandments hold before us the standards by which God would have us live, standards which have been established for our good. But, sad to say, it is not hard to see when looking at our lives against the Ten Commandments that we have often gone far wide of the mark. In other words, when we compare our lives against the standards of the Ten Commandments, we see that we have sinned.

Looking at such a reflection can easily make one feel depressed. That, however, is not what God wants. Instead God wants us to become ever sensitive to our needs for help and forgiveness, which He Himself is eager to provide. This is how that works; this is how our need is identified and how it is met.

❖ ❖ ❖ ❖ ❖

Some people say that while there is only one god, he/she/it goes by many names. Therefore, even though we pray to and worship God by different names, it is all the same god. What do you think about that?

❖ ❖ ❖ ❖ ❖

Commandment 1: "You shall have no other gods."

Martin Luther then asks: "What does this mean?"

And the answer: "We should fear, love, and trust in God above all things."

All of that brings us back to our opening question: "Who is God?" Who is this God whom we should fear, love, and trust above all else? (Remember, the question is not "Is there a god?" but "Who is God?")

❖ ❖ ❖ ❖ ❖

In the ancient Hebrew language, only consonants were used — no vowels. The four consonants, called the Tetragrammaton, used to spell God's name are Y H W H. Adding the vowels, the word is Yahweh, which comes from the Hebrew word which means "to be," a verb. Since the ancient Hebrews were very concerned about not using God's name, Yahweh, carelessly when referring to God, they would substitute the name Adonai, which means "Lord." When you take the consonants Y H W H and interpose the vowels of Adonai, A O A (dropping the I), through the process of transliteration you arrive at the hybrid word J(Y) a h o v(w) a h, Jehovah.

❖ ❖ ❖ ❖ ❖

That second question has always really been the first question: "Who is God?" When God approached Moses in the Wilderness of Sinai and told him to go back to Egypt in order to lead the Children of Israel out of that foreign land into the Promised Land, Moses responded by asking, "But whom shall I say sent me? Which god are you?" There certainly were a lot of gods circulating at that time. How was Moses to know, how were the Children of Israel to know, that He was the right One for the job?

God answered Moses by saying, "I am Who I am!" Interestingly enough, the word in the Hebrew language that God used to identify Himself ("Yahweh") is the verb "to be." Another way to look at it is to say that God is much like a verb — God, the right One, is a God of action. He does things.

❖ ❖ ❖ ❖ ❖
The verb/word "to be" implies action. Therefore, God is a God of actions. He initiates action. We also know people best by their actions (as well as by their size and how they look). Make a list of actions that well describe somebody you know. What do these actions have to say about that person? Make a list of actions that well describe God. What do the actions of God have to say about Him?
❖ ❖ ❖ ❖ ❖

After God put that straight with Moses, He proceeded to give more details, more information, on Who He was, saying, "Tell the people that I AM He who is the God of your fathers, Abraham, Isaac, and Jacob. I AM He who called Abraham out of the Ur of the Chaldees. I AM the One who led him to Canaan. I AM the One who gave him Isaac as a son. I AM the One who gave Jacob as a son to Isaac. I AM the One who gave twelve sons to Jacob, one of whom was named Joseph. I AM the One who went with Joseph to Egypt. I AM the One who blessed him so that he rose to such a great position of power and influence in Egypt. And now I have seen the terrible calamity which has fallen upon my chosen people. Therefore, I have chosen you to go before them as my representative. You shall deliver them."

That is who God is!

Throughout the days of the Old Testament time God, He who was and is the only God, beside whom there is none other, kept on revealing Himself to His people through His acts, through what He was doing for them.

❖ ❖ ❖ ❖ ❖
The term "virtual reality" implies that something has existence if we think it does, even though it might not exist in fact — it cannot be proven. Does God exist because there are people who think that He does? Is His existence dependent upon people believing that He exists?

What are some examples of "virtual reality"? A French philosopher of a few centuries ago, Rene Descartes, said, "I think, therefore I am." Do you think that something exists, even yourself, purely because you think it?

❖ ❖ ❖ ❖ ❖

We, the people of the New Testament, also do not have to debate the question, "Is there a god?" (Debating the question doesn't make it so or not so anyway.) But our real concern still is, "Who is God?" Whom are we going to confess as our God? As in the old days so also in these days, there are a lot of gods competing for our allegiance. How can we find who is the right and true God?

❖ ❖ ❖ ❖ ❖

Limit yourself to the New Testament. What does it have to say about the nature of God?

❖ ❖ ❖ ❖ ❖

Again, the answer to that question is much like the answer to the question in Old Testament times. The answer rests in what God does, in that which He has done for us. There is ample evidence of what God has done for us. Think for a moment of Bethlehem. Think for another moment of Calvary. God certainly has made Himself known to us by what He has done, centering in Jesus, His coming to this earth and giving of His life on the cross.

John in the first chapter of his gospel writes:

In the beginning was the Word, and the Word was with God and the Word was God ...
And the Word became flesh and dwelt among us, and we beheld His glory, glory as of
the only begotten of the Father full of grace and truth.

These words tell us that we know God in and through Jesus. He is the God we all need to know. "For there is no other name under heaven, given among men, whereby we must be saved," proclaims the apostle Paul.

That brings us back to home base: "You shall have no other gods." God has not given us that commandment because He is jealous of other gods — because He is worried about competition from them. Other gods are merely figments of our imaginations anyway. But God is "jealous" of us. He loves us so much that He wants us to love Him the same way. Thus He has given us this as the first Commandment, because He knows that there are no other gods that we need. The God of which we have need is the God who forgives us our sins and restores us in that image in which He had originally created us.

❖ ❖ ❖ ❖ ❖
The word "jealous" has a background that includes the idea of "zeal," which is related to enthusiasm and intense concern. Does that help you to understand the use of "jealous" when speaking about God? Does that understanding of "jealous" help you to appreciate what it means to be forgiven and what is necessary for forgiveness to happen? Who, what kind of God, can do what we need the most?
❖ ❖ ❖ ❖ ❖

Yes, that is our greatest need: to be forgiven so that we can be restored. We have need of a God who can do this, who can get the job done. There is only One who can, and He is ours.

❖ ❖ ❖ ❖ ❖
It has been said that nothing happens which is not "need motivated." For example, we go to bed, because we have a need to sleep. We get up, because we have a need to get moving again. What are some of your important needs? What is your most important need? Does God have needs? What is one of His most important needs? Why do you think it is so important?
❖ ❖ ❖ ❖ ❖

Martin Luther in his *Large Catechism* asks the question: "What does it mean to have a God?" True to form he also presents the answer: "To have a God is to have someone or something to which we look for all good and in which we find help for every time of need." God then is He who is above everything else in life, who is most important in life, and who also guides the way one lives his life. Because of that, the First Commandment is absolutely necessary if all the others are going to have any meaning or value. There just is no sense in listening to His voice above all other voices unless He is Number One.

Some people might think that all of this is rather selfish on the part of God. If any person that you know said those things and demanded the attention that God does, you would consider him or her to be rather arrogant and conceited. Why should you let God get away with it? For this very reason: God wants you to have Him first in your heart because He has you first in His heart. Even as He first loved you so He wants you to love Him.

How can you best love God?

Obviously, by receiving from Him the gift that He wants so much to give to you — the gift of His grace and mercy, His forgiveness, which is His love.

But there is more: we also honor God by reflecting that image of His love which He has placed into our hearts. The First Commandment is well kept when we do, in God's name, what He has done for us. That means when in the name of God made flesh, in the name of Jesus, we love our fellow man, when we love one another as we have been loved, that then we are doing exactly what the First Commandment expects.

❖ ❖ ❖ ❖ ❖

Above all, God is love. (See 1 John 1, and especially 1 John 4:8.) When it comes to real love, who initiates the action? The one loved? Or the one loving? What does that have to say about our relationship with God? What does that have to say about our following the example of God in the Flesh, Jesus? What is your neighbor's (the person next to you at home, at church, at school, at work) greatest need? What can you do to meet that need?

❖ ❖ ❖ ❖ ❖

Jesus, shortly before His crucifixion, was talking to His disciples about this. You can find the entire account in Matthew 25. The long and the short of it is summarized when He said:

I was hungry and you fed me. I was thirsty and you gave me drink. Cold, in need of shelter, sick, lonely, and you gave me clothing to wear, you took me in, you visited me, you comforted me ... Whenever you do this for any one of your brothers or sisters in need, you do it as if it was for me.

There is more involved here than just concern for food and drink, for clothing and friendship. For if we really love our neighbor as we have been loved, then we will also do for him as God has done for us, and that certainly includes our willingness to be forgiving.

So it is that "Love God" is and must be the First Commandment if all the others are going to make any sense and if the rest are going to work. How we live is all dependent upon how God lives for us. That gives us the power to live like Him for others. And when we come up short of always having God first in our lives, when the First Commandment shows us once again our sin, it also reminds us once again of the greatness of God who is even willing to forgive us for that. And that, after all, is our greatest need, and that forgiveness comes only from Him who loves the world so much that He gave for it His only begotten Son.

Questions

1. When we say the Commandments are like a "curb," what do we mean?

2. When we say the Commandments are like a "mirror," what do we mean?

3. "Who" did God say to Moses He was?

4. What do we mean when we say that "God is a verb"?

5. How does God reveal Himself to us?

6. What does God done for us?

7. What does it mean to have a God?

8. Because He first loved us God wants us to _____ Him.

9. How can we best love God?

Discussion

1. Is the real issue these days not so much setting up a false god, but having no god at all?

2. Discuss replacing a God outside of oneself with a god within oneself.

The Ten Commandments:
The Second Commandment

❖ ❖ ❖ ❖ ❖
Names usually are nouns. But many nouns have verbal roots; they come from verbs. For example, the common noun "automobile" means "something that runs by itself," and the proper noun "Kristen" means "one who is (acts) like Christ." In fact, all nouns can trace their heritage to some verb. Use your imagination and translate a few nouns (common and proper) into action words. But sometimes nouns lose their connection with their verbal roots. What are some examples of that (both common and proper)? For example, the word "seal" (referring to that furry animal that lives in the ocean) originally meant to "draw or pull something along," like drawing your finger over an edge of an envelope to seal it. That is how seals move on land. How about some proper names? Does Timothy always "fear God"?
❖ ❖ ❖ ❖ ❖

My name is David. And that is what I would like to talk to you about. Not my name "David," but about names.

Names are important. We really don't know anything or anybody without giving it, her, him, a name. Even this book has a name so that it can be identified from all the other hundreds, thousands, even millions of other books that have been written.

Names, however, not only identify: they also describe. This "Catechism Companion," for example, is a book which addresses itself to the Christian faith as seen through the eyes of a Lutheran pastor as it has been learned from another book, that one written by Dr. Martin Luther and known as the *Small Catechism*. I am sure that both Martin Luther's name and the words "small" and "catechism" tell us a lot about the nature of that book.

When children are born, one of the most frequently asked questions is, "What is going to be his/her name?" A child must have a name to be somebody. When Elizabeth, Zechariah's wife, gave birth to her first and only son, some thought that he should be named after his father, Zechariah. That would be nice. But when Zechariah, who, from the time that the angel had told him that he would have a son whose name was to be John, had been without the ability to speak, suddenly was able to talk again, he said, "The child's name shall be John." The name "John" means "God is good; God is gracious." Certainly God was good, granting to this elderly, childless couple a son, the very one who would prepare the way for the Messiah. Yes, "The child's name shall be John." He has come to be known to us today as "John the Baptist." That was his name, and that is what he did. That was his reputation.

You see, one of the most important functions of a name is that of bearing a person's reputation — just like John who became known as a "baptizer."

❖ ❖ ❖ ❖ ❖

Names carry our reputations. If we are honest about it, the names that we often like the best are names by which we knew people whose reputations were good. What are some of your favorite names? Of whom do they remind you?

❖ ❖ ❖ ❖ ❖

I am also reminded of another person's name. This one is "Aldonza." She is a character in Cervantes' *Don Quixote (The Man of La Mancha).* In that story, Don Quixote, wandering through the Spanish countryside, thinking that he is a great knight, dueling with windmills because he is nearsighted and thinks that they are the enemy, comes one night to an inn which he mistakes for a castle. Now this is no ordinary inn. It is more like a brothel of which one "Aldonza" is the mistress. But Don Quixote, seeing things only the way he can see things, views Aldonza as a noble lady and so calls her "Dulcinea." Her name is changed from "Aldonza," which means "One who shamelessly gives herself away," to "Dulcinea," which means "One who is sweetness and innocence."

Through the rest of the story Dulcinea struggles with her new name, resisting what it implies. But the man of La Mancha, Don Quixote, persists in calling her "Dulcinea," and slowly but surely the names has a transforming effect upon her until finally, as Don Quixote is dying, she simply says, "My name is Dulcinea." What new power and beauty she found in that name.

❖ ❖ ❖ ❖ ❖

Although we often distance ourselves from what our names really mean, nicknames frequently have an influence upon how we behave. If somebody calls you "cutie," you might very well act in a coy and shy way, rather than in a boisterous and rude fashion. If somebody calls you "stupid," you probably will have the tendency to act that way. Identify some nicknames that have influenced the behavior of some people you know.

❖ ❖ ❖ ❖ ❖

No wonder God in the Second Commandment says, "Be careful how you use my name ... You shall not misuse the name of the Lord your God."

In Old Testament times the Israelites were so conscious of possibly misusing God's name that they substituted another name for it. God had revealed himself to Moses as "Yahweh." The name simply means "I Am." God is saying, "I Am the God who Is." He is the only God who has existence. I Am, He Is, the origin of all that is! Thus "Yahweh" is the proper name of God.

However, when the Second Commandment came along, it made the Israelites so afraid of taking God's name in vain, saying it carelessly or without thinking (misusing it), that they decided not to use it at all. Therefore, they substituted for it the name "Adonai," which means "Lord" or "Leader." Thus, whenever a Hebrew would read in the Scriptures the word "Yahweh," he would substitute for it the word "Adonai."

❖ ❖ ❖ ❖ ❖
Look back to the previous chapter and its discussion on the name of God.
❖ ❖ ❖ ❖ ❖

It is also interesting to note that originally Hebrew words were written only with consonants, no vowels. However, when the Old Testament was translated into the English language in the sixteenth and seventeenth centuries leading up to the publication of the King James Version of the Bible in 1611, the consonants of Yahweh (Y-H-W-H) were put together with the vowels of Adonai (A-O-A-I) and the result was our artificial English word "Jehovah."

The important thing to remember, however, is not whether we say "Yahweh" or "Adonai" or "Lord" or simply "God," But that His name is said in such a way that it reflects His reputation and His influence among us.

❖ ❖ ❖ ❖ ❖
What does the way you use God's name have to say about your relationship with God?
❖ ❖ ❖ ❖ ❖

"You shall not misuse the name of the Lord your God."

"What does this mean?" Martin Luther asks in the *Small Catechism*.

We should fear and love God so that we do not curse, swear, use satanic arts, lie, or deceive by His name, but call upon it in every trouble, pray, praise, and give thanks.

There are two important things to note here: 1) How we should not use God's name, and 2) What good use to which we should employ it.

❖ ❖ ❖ ❖ ❖
Just about everything in this world has a positive and a negative side (opposites). Sometimes that is called "Yin and Yang." That also has to do with our behavior. There is good behavior and there is negative behavior. Nothing is neutral. So also with the words we speak. What are some examples of words being put to both good and bad use?
❖ ❖ ❖ ❖ ❖

First: How not to use it. Using God's name carelessly is sometimes referred to as using it "in vain." The word "vain" simply means "empty, without meaning." In other words, God is saying, "Don't use my name if you don't mean it." Many times we hear people exclaim without thinking, "Oh, my God," or perhaps they just say "God." The name is used like a punctuation mark. When those who speak this way are reminded that they have used God's name in vain, they might very well respond by saying, "Oh, I didn't really mean anything by it ... It's just an expression." But that is precisely what God is speaking about when He says, "Don't use my name in vain. Don't use it unless you really mean it."

Now, I am not advocating cursing, but usually when a person uses God's name to damn something at least he or she means it. There is power in those words. But simply to say "God" without meaning it, that is the height of vainness, emptiness; that is one of the worst ways to misuse it. If you don't mean it, then don't say it.

❖ ❖ ❖ ❖ ❖
Vanity is emptiness. It is hollow. But it is not meaningless. It is not neutral. What are some words (expressions) which are sometimes said which we don't really mean, but which have meaning when they are heard by others?
❖ ❖ ❖ ❖ ❖

There are many times, however, when we do well to mean it. And this is the positive side of the commandment. "Call upon (it) me (my name) in the day of trouble; I will deliver you, and you shall glorify me" (Psalm 50:15). "Pray, praise, and give thanks." God wants to hear from us. He wants us to talk with Him when things are bothering us, just as children at times like to speak to their fathers.

❖❖❖❖❖
Solitary confinement is considered by many to be the worst kind of punishment, because there is no opportunity to talk with anyone. So also "the silent treatment" is one of the cruelest ways in which we can treat another person. What are some important things to talk about at home among family members? What are some of the important things to talk about with those with whom you work, or with those with whom you go to school? Can you think of any other such kinds of situations in which it is important to talk to each other? Why then does God want to hear from us even if He already knows what is on our minds?
❖❖❖❖❖

The Germans have borrowed from the people of Jesus' day the custom of teaching their children to begin their prayers with the words "Abba Vater" (Dear Father). The idea is that we are to call upon God because we trust Him and know that even as He wants to hear from us, His dear children, so also as our dear Father He is wanting to do for us what is good for us.

In addition to just turning to God with our problems, He also likes to hear from us when things are going well. Fathers don't like to talk to their children only when there are problems. They like to hear about the good things, too. That is all part of a healthy relationship between children and their fathers. So we also address God, our Father, with our thanks. We tell Him about the good things which have made us happy.

There is one more point related to the Second Commandment that I would like to make. Anthropologists, those who study the history of human behavior, tell us that there are two things which make us distinct from all other creatures. One, as humans, we have opposing thumbs. That means that we can make things and pick them up with our hands and thus extend ourselves by means of our weapons and instruments (those things which we can make and pick up). And two, we also have a tongue, and that represents the gift of speech. No other creature can speak words, can make sentences, can affix symbols to objects and express itself creatively. Oh, yes, parrots and some other animals can make a variety of sounds and noises that might sound like words. But they can do that only as they are taught. They can only repeat what they have learned. But who has ever taught us all the millions of sentences we can make? Most of the sentences I have spoken today I have never said before. Most of these sentences which you have just read you have never seen before. But because of the gift of speech, we can create hundreds, thousands, yes even millions and billions of sentences, new sentences never before said or written.

❖❖❖❖❖
The ability to communicate is a creative ability. Consider and discuss with someone the role communicating has had in the development of civilization. How important is the communication industry to our society today? However, why is it sometimes "message sent not message received"?
❖❖❖❖❖

The ability to speak is sometimes considered to be the greatest of all human skills, because by it we can express ourselves, we can extend ourselves, and we can influence others for good or for ill. This ability is ever creative. The point is: to what better use can this tremendous power be employed than to use it in the giving of praise to God who is the author and creator of all that is? Indeed, man's greatest honor is that he might honor God with his speech. His gift of speech, the employment of words, knows no higher level than to be used in praising God.

❖ ❖ ❖ ❖ ❖

If praising God is such an important function of human speech, what effect should that have on a congregation's gathering for worship? If praising God is such an important activity in eternity, what effect should that have upon a congregation's worship service? What then, do you think, is the chief reason for worshiping?

❖ ❖ ❖ ❖ ❖

The Book of Revelation, that last and the only prophetic book in the New Testament, which presents to us all sorts of symbolic pictures of eternity, also gives us brief glimpses of the angels and saints in heaven gathered before the throne of God. And what are they doing there? They are singing, singing God's praises!

Holy, Holy, Holy, is the Lord, the Almighty ... Blessing and glory and wisdom and thanksgiving and honor and power and might be to our God forever and ever.

I don't know if the only thing we are going to be doing in heaven is singing, but this I do know — the only pictures of heaven which we have been given in advance present to us just how important God considers our praises to be. The only pictures of the angels and the saints of heaven that we have show them singing. And that, I think, is the ultimate way in which we will have the privilege of "keeping" the Second Commandment.

Questions

1. What does your name mean?

2. What is one of the most important things a name does?

3. What does "Yahweh" mean?

4. What does "Adonai" mean?

5. How should we not use God's name?

6. What is the height of "vainness" in using God's name?

7. What does "Abba" mean?

8. What two things make us different from all other creatures?

9. What is the finest way we can use our gift of speech?

10. In the Book of Revelation what are the saints doing?

Discussion

1. Think of someone who has "lived up to his or her name." Discuss how that person's name has defined his or her life.

2. Discuss some practical and everyday ways in which God's name can be kept holy by you.

The Ten Commandments:
The Third Commandment

❖ ❖ ❖ ❖ ❖
Sometimes things are "first" because they happened first, like Sunday is the first day of the week. It comes before the rest. Some things are "first" because they are that which is most important, like Sunday being the most important day of the week. Do you think that Sunday is the most important day of the week? If so, why? If not so, why? If not so, what day would you say is the most important of all?
❖ ❖ ❖ ❖ ❖

"Remember the Sabbath day by keeping it holy."

And "What does this mean?"

"We should fear and love God that we may not despise preaching and His Word, but hold it sacred and gladly hear and learn it."

In some respects we might think that the Third Commandment should be the First Commandment. This is why: when God finished creating the world in six days (Genesis 1), it is said that He rested on the seventh day. He rested from all that He had done. Therefore, God set aside the seventh day of the week as a day to "be hallowed"; it was a day to be made holy, and that means that it was to be different from all other days.

You might wonder, "Why did God rest?" Was He tired from making the heavens and the earth? Was He all worn out? Did He have to catch His breath before He could continue with running what He had created?

Of course not! Instead, the key to the answer to why He found it necessary to rest on the seventh day and then set it aside to be also for us a day of rest can be found in something He said immediately before He had created man and woman, Adam and Eve. He said, "Let us make them in our image, so that they will have dominion over all creation." In other words, Adam and Eve, men and women, were (are) to be God's representatives.

It is generally agreed that among the best ways to teach behavior and values is by setting an example. It is foolish to say, "Do as I say, not as I do." It is wiser to say, "Do as I say, and as I do." What are some of the positive things you have learned in life from those who have set for you a good example? Recall also examples of those who have said one thing but done another. What kind of impression have they left on you? In your own life, what opportunities do you have to set a good example for others?

In order for them to do the rather awesome job of managing all of creation, so that they might be its caretakers, God gave them an example. He rested on the seventh day in order to emphasize that if those who were created in His image were going to be able to do a good job with the assignment He had given to them, they would have to follow His example and find rest and refreshment in the Sabbath Day. In other words, the day of Sabbath rest was key to all of the other days of the week. If the six were going to go as God had wished them to go, the seventh would have to be set aside and be honored as He had originally planned.

Even though this commandment is not the first of the ten, I think that it is central to all of them. In fact, it is central to life. If our lives are going to go according to the way God wills them to go, if we are going to be up to the challenges and tasks which He presents to us, we must find our center in Him. In Him we must find our rest and refreshment.

Lives which have something central to them are lives which seem to have a focus. There are, however, usually numerous things which compete for being the central focus. What are some of the things which do such competing in your life? Make a list of them and rate them on a scale of 1 to 10, 10 being the most important. After you have done that, take the five that you rated the highest. Now, put them in order with number 1 being the most important of the five. What does that tell you about the focus of your life? Are you happy with your focus? Do you think it should be changed somewhat?

A number of years ago I went to Germany. Among many other things which I noticed, this was inescapable: central to all German villages, towns, and even large cities are the churches. And even though many of these houses of worship are now 1,000 years old, they still stand tall in the center of things. Before skyscrapers were invented, nothing ever towered above the church's steeple. It was always the highest structure in town. All eyes could see it. Without a doubt, the churches were at the center of the lives of the people who lived in those places; their churches stood tall over their living. Their churches, their houses of worship, were those points at the center of their communities around which their lives revolved.

❖ ❖ ❖ ❖ ❖

How central or important is church (your congregation, going to church, church activities) to you? If you find that it is important, identify reasons why it is. If you find that it is not so important, identify reasons why it is not. What would or could make church more central to your life? Would you like it to be more central, more of a focus for your life?

❖ ❖ ❖ ❖ ❖

Much blessed are you if you find that your church, your house of worship and all that is connected with that, is central to your life. Our churches don't have to be the tallest buildings in town; they don't have to tower over skyscrapers. That is not necessary. Many of them aren't even in the center of town. Yet the idea persists that our places of worship, where we gather together with other people of God as the family of faith to have our lives rested and refreshed in the Lord, that place, that holy ground, which has been sanctified for that purpose, should be central to our lives.

That is what is meant by "Remember the Sabbath day by keeping it holy."

❖ ❖ ❖ ❖ ❖

There are many important moments in history. What would you include in the top five? Make sure you have good reasons for selecting these five. In your own life, what do you think are the five most important events? Be sure also to give good reasons for selecting these five. Sometimes it is difficult to choose one of the five as the most important. If you can do that, what would be the number 1 event from both of these lists?

❖ ❖ ❖ ❖ ❖

Here we must pause for a little footnote: Sometimes the question is raised, "But if God appointed the seventh day as the Sabbath Day, why do so many worship on the first day, on Sunday, instead of on Saturday?" Well, I don't know if the Lord is going to argue too loud and too long with us over which day is the better and more proper day for the Sabbath. The point is: Do it! Make sure that each week you find your rest and refreshment in God so that you indeed can be the kind of representative on earth of Him that He had planned you to be.

❖ ❖ ❖ ❖ ❖
Refer to the earlier section which discusses things which are "first." In Genesis 1 the first commandment given to humankind really was, "Be fruitful, multiply, subdue the earth and have dominion over it." The Second Commandment was to observe the seventh day as a day of rest so that the First Commandment could be properly handled. Now the Christian church has decided that the first day of the week would be a better day as the Sabbath Day. Do you think this choice was a good one? Think again about things which are most important. What is most important for the Christian faith? From what event in history does everything else flow?
❖ ❖ ❖ ❖ ❖

But as for the first day as our Sabbath: Christians worship on Sunday, the first day of the week. That tradition goes all the way back to the custom of the disciples of Christ themselves. They gathered, we are told in the Book of the Acts of the Apostles, on the first day of the week in order to honor the Lord's resurrection, which took place on the first day of the week. Thus, they begin each week with their remembering Christ's victory over sin, death, and the devil. To them that triumph was the most important moment in all of history. It was the most important thing that ever happened. It was the focal point of all time. Christ's resurrection was like a new creation. It was like the start of a new time. And it was from that they drew strength for their living. So they began the new week in worship. Worshiping on Sunday is an apostolic tradition.

In Acts 2:42 we have a rather significant look into the life of the early Christian church and what it was like. Luke writes: "And they devoted themselves to the Apostles' teaching, and fellowship, and the breaking of bread and prayers." What those words tell us is that these people came together often, devoutly and religiously, in order to gather around the Word (the studying of the Scriptures); they came together often for fellowship (enjoying each other's company); they celebrated the breaking of the bread (participating in Holy Communion, even as Jesus said, "Do this in remembrance of me"); and they were faithful in praying for each other.

❖ ❖ ❖ ❖ ❖
What are some of the activities that take place at your church on Sunday? Which of these do you think are important? Which are not so important? Use the reference to the four activities characteristic of the early church recorded in Acts 2:42. What are some of the other activities that are characteristic of an ordinary Sabbath day for you? Which of these activities are important, and which are not so important? Make sure you have good reasons to support your choices.

It is good when all four of these ingredients are incorporated into our remembering the Sabbath Day to keep it holy. We do well when on our Sabbath we gather together around the Word, are supportive of each other, celebrate Holy Communion as a remembrance of Christ's resurrection, and pray for one another. That is good. That is very good! That is central to the Christian life.

Yes, I suppose that one can study the Word in private, can say his prayers in private, and can rest in private. But there is no substitute for coming together and sharing the goodness of God's grace. There simply is no substitute for assembling ourselves together on the Lord's Day to remember to keep it holy.

❖ ❖ ❖ ❖ ❖

When are some of the times that you prefer to be left alone? Why do you prefer at times to be left alone? What are some of the times when you feel lonely and wish that somebody was with you? What are some reasons why you would want someone to be with you?

It is said that solitary confinement is one of the worst forms of punishment. Some even think that it is torture. Why is that so?

When do you prefer to be alone at church? When do you prefer to have others around you at church? Who are some of the people at church to whom you feel closest? To whom would you like to feel closer? Are there any from whom you would like to keep your distance? Why?

❖ ❖ ❖ ❖ ❖

I conclude with a few words from Dietrich Bonhoeffer, one of my favorite writers. He was a pastor in Germany immediately before and during World War II. He was executed by the Nazis the day before the concentration camp into which he had been placed was liberated by the Allies. He knew firsthand what a blessing it was to be able to gather with fellow Christians around the Sacrament and Word of God. He also knew what a tragedy it was when that privilege was withheld.

It is by the grace of God that a congregation is permitted to gather visible in this world to share God's Word and sacrament. Not all Christians receive this blessing. The imprisoned, the sick, the scattered lonely, the proclaimers of the Gospel in (far away) lands stand alone. They know that visible fellowship is a blessing. They remember, as the Psalmist did, how they went "with the multitude ... to the house of God, with the voice of joy and praise, with a multitude that kept holyday" (Psalm 42:4) ...

So the physical presence of other Christians is a source of incomparable joy and strength to the believer ...

The believer feels no shame, as though he were still living too much in the flesh, when he yearns for the physical presence of other Christians. Man was created a body, the Son of God appeared on earth in the body, he was raised in the body, in the sacrament the believer receives the Lord Christ in the body, and the resurrection of the dead will bring about the perfected fellowship of God's spiritual-physical creatures. The believer therefore lauds the creator, the Redeemer, God, Father, Son and Holy Spirit, for the bodily presence of a brother. The prisoner, the sick person, the Christian in exile sees in the companionship of a fellow Christian a physical sign of the gracious presence of the triune God. Visitor and visited in loneliness recognize in each other the Christ who is present in the body. They receive and meet each other as one meets the Lord, in reverence, humility, and joy ...

It is easily forgotten that the fellowship of Christian brethren is a gift of grace, a gift of the kingdom of God that any day may be taken from us, that the time that still separates us from utter loneliness may be brief indeed. Therefore, let him who until now has had the privilege of living a common Christian life with other Christians praise God's grace from the bottom of his heart. Let him thank God on his knees and declare: It is grace, nothing but grace, that we are allowed to live in community with Christian brethren. (Dietrich Bonhoeffer, *Life Together*: Chapter One, "Community." Used by permission.)

Questions

1. Why could the Third Commandment be considered the First Commandment?

2. Why was the seventh day set aside by God?

3. What does it mean to be made in the image of God?

4. Why must we find rest and refreshment on the Sabbath?

5. What is central to most German towns?

6. What should be central to our lives?

7. Why do we worship on the first day of the week instead of on the seventh?

8. In Acts 2:42, what four things did the early Christians do?
   a.
   b.
   c.
   d.

9. Why is it important to worship together?

Discussion

1. The use of God's name is central to both the Second and the Third Commandments. Show how this is so.

2. Life can be enriched or impoverished, all depending upon our use of the Sabbath Day. Discuss how that can be so.

The Ten Commandments:
The Fourth Commandment

❖ ❖ ❖ ❖ ❖
Our lives are defined by the relationships we have. My father used to tell me that you could tell very much about a person by the friends the person had (relationships). What would others know about you by knowing about your friends?

How we treat those who are around us (even the dog and the cat) also tells a lot about what kind of persons we are. What do you think people know about you based on how you treat others? What do you think others think about you based on how you get along with the members of your family? How important is it for you to get along with the members of your family? Why do you feel that way?
❖ ❖ ❖ ❖ ❖

"Honor your father and your mother."

Our look at the Ten Commandments, inscribed by God's fiery finger into two tablets of stone on Mount Sinai and then delivered to the people of God by Moses, brings us to the Fourth Commandment. With it also begins the second table of the law. The first three commandments make up the first table of the law. Those commandments directed our attention to our relationship with God. The First Commandment: God is to be first in our lives. The Second Commandment: we are to honor His name. The Third Commandment: it is He whom we are to worship regularly, finding in Him our rest and refreshment.

Now we begin the second table: it contains seven commandments and directs our attention to our relationship with others, with one another. Basic to all of this is how we get along with the members of our families, and that is the subject of the Fourth Commandment: the family, the foundation upon which society is built.

Honor your father and mother.

What does this mean? We should fear and love God so that we do not despise or anger our parents and other authorities, but honor them, serve and obey them, love and cherish them.

When I review the Ten Commandments with the youth in my catechism classes, I hint that they may find this commandment the most difficult of all to keep. Actually, all the commandments are difficult to keep; in fact, it is impossible for anyone to keep them perfectly. We all have to confess with the Apostle Paul that we "daily sin much, not doing the good we should be doing, and spending way too much time doing what we ought not to be doing."

❖ ❖ ❖ ❖ ❖

We all have different reasons for having our problems with keeping the various ten commandments. Which one do you have a particularly difficult time keeping? Why do you think that is so?

❖ ❖ ❖ ❖ ❖

When I suggest that the Fourth Commandment may be the most difficult of all to keep (especially for children), I mean this: it is not always easy to love, honor, and respect parents. After all, mothers and fathers are often at great odds with their children. Children and parents often do not think alike. Parents like to have things, including those little ones (children), under control. Meanwhile, children growing up, flexing their wills and independence, often challenge their parents' authority. Children have been doing that ever since there were children. All who are mothers or fathers were once upon a time sons or daughters, and I am sure that at one time or the other — perhaps at many times — they found it difficult to "honor, serve, obey, love, and cherish" their fathers and mothers.

❖ ❖ ❖ ❖ ❖

Relationships between family members often become strained. What are some of the reasons why that is so? When that happens, what can be done to make things better? There have been all sorts of books written about how to structure relationships between parents and children. Describe some of these systems. What do you think makes for healthy relationships between parents and children?

❖ ❖ ❖ ❖ ❖

Therefore, we have the Fourth Commandment. But does that mean that God gave it to us in order to keep the lid on things? To keep order in the family? To keep society somewhat civilized? To legitimize power and authority in the hands of parents?

If that is what we think, if that is the real reason why we have it, then children really lose out in the deal, that is, if from God Himself there seems to be coming a word which orders that children be kept under the thumb. I don't think, however, that the main reason the Fourth Commandment has been given is just to keep children in check and under control, as important as that may be. For if that is what this commandment is all about then it is just another sociological guideline invented by people, with nothing divine about it at all.

Therefore, I ask you again, is the purpose of the Fourth Commandment principally and primarily to keep order at home and in society?

I don't think so. I think there is something far more profound here. Saint Paul wrote in his letter to the Ephesians in chapters 5 and 6 how Christians are to get along with one another. (In these chapters he includes his commentary on the Fourth Commandment: "Children, obey your parents in the Lord, for this is right. 'Honor your father and your mother that it may be well with you and that you may live long on the earth.' ") In verse 21 of chapter 5 he also writes these key words: "Be subject to one another out of reverence for Christ."

❖ ❖ ❖ ❖ ❖
Ephesians 5:21 is a key verse for structuring Christian relationships. What is the essence of what Paul is saying in this verse? How does that apply to the relationships between husbands and wives, parents and children, and employers and employees? If we all lived according to the principle of this verse, how do you imagine the world would be?
❖ ❖ ❖ ❖ ❖

These words immediately precede that entire portion of this letter in which Paul gives instructions to the Ephesians (and to us) about how husbands and wives, parents and children, even employers and employees are to treat one another. In other words, the words "be subject to one another out of reverence for Christ" apply to how we treat one another. Everyone who is in Christ (all Christians) ought to be, out of reverence for Christ, subject to one another, which means that we ought to place ourselves in service to one another.

You see, in this old world of ours everybody wants to be the one who is served. Getting all of that attention makes us think that we really are somebody. It's a sign of power for a people who are riddled with insecurities. Therefore, we like to be the ones who are the receivers of honor and respect. We like it when others give us the things that we want. We like it when we have things our way. This world of ours puts a premium on that. That seems to be what everybody is striving for. No wonder then that so many husbands want their wives to wait on them. No wonder so many wives also try to manipulate and control their husbands. No wonder parents want obedience from their children. It's a matter of control, you see. No wonder children as they grow older think that it is so important to flex their independence and free themselves from the control of their parents. That is an important sign of growing up; it is important to their self-esteem. No wonder then that many think that life is little more than a struggle for power, a struggle to free oneself from the power of others and the struggle to have power over others. That even is characteristic of many relationships between employer and employee.

> **The struggle for power seems to be an age-old preoccupation of humankind. What are some of the power struggles that you see going on around you at school or work, in your neighborhood or in your community at large? Why do you think people want power over others? Martin Luther said that as Christians we are "lords over all, yet slaves to all." What do you think he meant by those words? Apply Philippians 2:5-8 to this.**

Meanwhile, Paul says: "Everybody, especially those of you who are in Christ, place yourself in service to the other person." Put him, her, them first and yourself last, at the end of the line. Live to serve others instead of thinking that "this is really living" when they serve you.

Only those who are "in Christ," who live the Christ-like life, are those who can really place themselves into that kind of service of others. You see, the essence of Christ's life was love and forgiveness, and that is the ultimate in service. It is only when we love and forgive one another that we can put the other person first and ourselves last.

Now let's see how that works itself out with children who have an ear for what the Fourth Commandment says. Not all children have parents who do very much to warrant, to merit, their respect and honor. We often hear it said about somebody who should be receiving honor and respect but who doesn't get it, "They haven't earned it." But, you see, in Christ there is no need to earn it. Love, honor, and respect in Christ are always given. It does not have to be earned. It is always a gift.

> **It has often been said that respect (honor) is something that must be earned. What do you think about that? When respect (honor) is not earned but still given, what is the motivating power behind that? How/why can respect (honor) be given to those who do not deserve it? How important do you think it is to give it even if it is not earned? What must children do to their parents in order to respect them? Does that also work in the reverse: parents respecting their children? What must they do to their children before that can happen?**

A Christian family, then, is held together and can be a healthy family and can be a strong family (in spite of the quirks of its members, in spite of the tensions that might exist, and in spite of the downright out-and-out sins of children and parents) because and when children are able to forgive their parents because they love them. (Of course, that works in the reverse also: when parents are able to forgive their children because they love them.) That is when and how the Christian family is held together.

My father was a good man. I know of very few men who were better than he was. In some respects I can almost say that he earned and deserved my love, honor, and respect. In addition, I am sure that he was a far better father to me than what I often have been to my children. But I didn't love, honor, respect, and thus obey him because he earned it, or because I had to give it, but because in Christ I could always see him, my father, as God's good gift to me. In Christ, I like to see my children as gifts from God. In Christ, I hope that they see me as a gift from God.

Parents and children can look at each other as being gifts from God. What are some of the ways in which you can be a gift to your parents? What are some of the ways in which your parents have been a gift to you? On the other hand, sometimes parents hurt children and children hurt parents. Sometimes the hurt is small, and sometimes the hurt is big. When there is hurt, what can be done about it? How can it be handled? Is there ever any hurt which is just too big to handle? What can be done then?

In his explanation to the Fourth Commandment Luther writes, "We should fear and love God so that we do not despise or anger our parents and others in authority...." "Others in authority"? Who are they?

By "others in authority" Luther means those who occupy positions of respect and responsibility in society: for example, teachers and policemen. Speaking to those children gathered around his feet there in Wittenberg, Germany, Luther said that this commandment means that they, the children, should look at their teachers as gifts from God. That is hard for children to do sometimes, especially if they are not doing well at school. If school is unpleasant and the going is rough, it is all too easy to blame the teacher. Thus, the teacher is often looked upon as being the enemy instead of the friend. The teacher is then looked upon as being a bane rather than a blessing. I suppose that we could say the same thing about the police officer, especially if he has just issued us a ticket for speeding or caught us shoplifting. What makes matters even worse is if we know that in his or her private life that policeman or policewoman is anything but a model of virtue.

❖ ❖ ❖ ❖ ❖
> People who hold positions of authority in society can also be considered "gifts" from God. In what ways are public officials gifts from God? Some people even go so far as to say that "bad government is better than no government," meaning that having less than honorable public officials is better than having no public officials. What do you think about that? Would you be able to honor an openly evil person who is in a position of authority? Would you have been able to honor someone like Hitler or Stalin?

❖ ❖ ❖ ❖ ❖

In such situations it is difficult for any of us to look at teachers or policemen and so forth as being gifts from God. To complicate things even more, Luther also had in mind when referring to "other authorities" the boss at work. A gift from God? Hardly!

Yet in Christ the way we look at others changes. Now we live to serve. We are quick to forgive. We no longer need to challenge anybody and everybody. Consequently, we find that the quality of life is improved, enhanced, and God's most precious gift to us, the gift of life itself, is blessed again.

❖ ❖ ❖ ❖ ❖
> What is the one thing necessary for holding the world together for a Christian?

❖ ❖ ❖ ❖ ❖

Remember, the key to the Fourth Commandment is in the words "be subject to one another out of reverence for Christ." Children, treat your parents as Jesus would. And parents, treat your children as Jesus would. With the mind of Christ within us, out of reverence for Christ, we are called upon by this commandment to treat each other as Christ would treat us.

Questions

1. Where did God give the Ten Commandments?

2. How many Commandments are on the First Tablet?

3. What is their focus?

4. How many Commandments are on the Second Tablet?

5. What is their focus?

6. Why can we consider the Fourth Commandment the most difficult of all?

7. What is the "key" to the Fourth Commandment found in Ephesians 5:21?

8. Why does everybody try to control everybody else?

9. To whom is the Fourth Commandment primarily addressed?

10. Why give honor to parents?

11. Why is it no longer necessary when we are in Christ to earn respect?

12. What holds Christian families together?

13. In Christ we see each other as _____ from God.

14. Who are "other authorities"?

Discussion

1. Some think that the major problems we have in society today come from the breakdown of the family, which can also mean lack of respect for authority. What do you think? Back up what you think with supporting material.

2. Discuss ways in which the single parent family impacts on the Fourth Commandment and vice versa.

The Ten Commandments:
The Fifth Commandment

❖ ❖ ❖ ❖ ❖
Sometimes we hear it said, "Nothing seems to be sacred any more." What is meant by those words? What makes something sacred in the first place? What is the nature of something that is sacred? Are sacred things treated in any special way?
❖ ❖ ❖ ❖ ❖

"You shall not murder."

What does this mean? We should fear and love God so that we do not hurt or harm our neighbor in his body, but help and support him in every physical need.

There you have it: the Fifth Commandment and its explanation written by Dr. Martin Luther.

The Fifth Commandment has to do with the sacredness of life. Yes, life is sacred, especially human life, because (as the Scriptures declare to us) our lives come from God. God has breathed into us the very breath of life. In other words, we have within us the very breath of God. It comes from Him, is His, and we are His. Therefore, life is of great value.

❖ ❖ ❖ ❖ ❖
We live in a world which makes documentaries of serial killers, movie idols out of organized crime members, and heroes out of violent people. Crime seems to have gone from making the news to being entertainment. What kind of influence do you think that sort of thing has on our behavior? Do you think that the media (radio, television, the movies,

and the newspapers) merely report news, or do they also make news?
What do you think is the media's responsibility in this area?

❖ ❖ ❖ ❖ ❖

It is important for us to remember that, since today we live not merely on the edge of violence which treats life cheaply, but we live right in the midst of violence. Cities, once the havens of civilization, have so often become the wilderness of disorder. Ironic, isn't it, that now people often flee to the countryside for peace and safety, when not too long ago, it was in the city that security and protection could be found?

Not only have our cities become places of violence, but on every hand we are confronted by it. The news media present us with all too many gory details — riots, war, terrorism, murder, ritual slayings, and so forth. Yes, life, and especially human life, seems to be cheap these days, and very expendable, especially if it gets in the way. Today many lives can be quickly and easily put out of the way. For example, thousands of unborn babies, for convenience sake in the name of the right to choose, can be and are simply dismissed.

❖ ❖ ❖ ❖ ❖
Things which are cheap generally are treated in a careless manner. Name some things which are relatively cheap and which are handled accordingly. Do you think that there are some things in this world which simply are of more value than others? Do you think that some lives are of more value than others? Be sure that you are able to defend your position.
❖ ❖ ❖ ❖ ❖

At the other end of the spectrum of life, many of the aged who are no longer able to contribute much to their society are conveniently put out of the way, shoved in a corner. Yes, they may still be fed and clothed, but all too often they also become and are left unloved.

Perhaps the cheapness of life is also compounded by all the stories we have heard about mass killings and serial killers. Our curiosities seem to be pricked by all the sordid details. It almost appears as if there is competition to see who can kill the most, or who can invent a method for killing that is more bizarre than the next.

❖ ❖ ❖ ❖ ❖
There are a number of reasons why we live in a violent society. List as many of them as you can, and explain why they have contributed to the problem of violence. What do you think is at the root of violence? What is its prime cause?
❖ ❖ ❖ ❖ ❖

After having heard the stories of the millions killed by the Nazis and the Communists during the time of the Second World War, and after having heard of more recent wars of genocide in Africa, Southeast Asia, and Eastern Europe, it is almost easy to become numb to these tragedies. Life, in spite of the fact that it comes from God, seems to be so dispensable.

Making this situation even worse is the fact that the cheapness of life and its dispensability seem to be promoted by much of what is presented to us by the entertainment media. For example, both the daytime and the nighttime "soaps" portray people using and abusing one another in rather merciless and pitiful ways. Add to that all the violence that is worked upon another person which is at the center of so many films and other television programs these days. We like to complain a lot about pornography. The "pornography" of violence is just as bad, and even more deadly than the pornography of sex.

It is for such reasons as those that the Fifth Commandment tells us that we should never do anything which would hurt or harm our neighbor in any physical way.

You see, every human being carries the stamp, the image, of the Almighty. In every other person's eyes, in every other person's face, we ought to be able to see the eyes and the face of God. And when we intentionally maim or hurt or harm or kill our neighbor, when we intentionally injure him in any way, we inflict a wound upon the very heart of God. When we treat each other that way, we are saying, "You are in my way. You are dispensable. You are of no value. I wish that you were not, that you did not exist. I don't want you to be a part of my world."

❖ ❖ ❖ ❖ ❖

Do you agree or disagree with the statement that when you injure another person you inflict a wound on God? What are some of the ways in which God feels pain and hurt?

❖ ❖ ❖ ❖ ❖

Ultimately, ending another person's life ends the possibility of our ever having something to do with that person again. That person simply ceases to exist for us. Therefore, both the Scriptures and Luther said that we ought not even to hate another person. The Old Testament law specifically said that one ought not to hate his neighbor. Jesus even went so far as to include with our "neighbors" our enemies. We are not even allowed to hate them. Because, you see, hating is like killing. Hating is also saying, "I never want to have anything to do with you again." Hating is saying, "You are dead to me." No wonder the Scriptures say, "Anyone who hates his brother is a murderer" (1 John 3:15), and "He who does not love his brother whom he has seen, cannot love God whom he has not seen" (1 John 4:20). If the image of God in our brother is destroyed, if in his eyes and face we can no longer see God, then God is dead too! Then God is dead to us.

❖ ❖ ❖ ❖ ❖

Hatred is about as strong of a negative feeling that is possible. Try to picture hatred. What color would it be? What shape would it be? Are there some things that should be hated? Can you ever hate gracefully? Sometimes we might be called upon to hate and love at the same time. Can you imagine what such circumstances might be?

The entire first letter of John focuses on loving God and one's neighbor. It is not a long book in the Bible. Read the entire epistle of 1 John now. After you have completed that, what one thought surfaces to the top of your mind?

❖ ❖ ❖ ❖ ❖

So, the Fifth Commandment ought to be taken very seriously, because behind it, behind every life, is the breath of God.

Will Rogers, the American humorist and author, once said, "I never met a man I didn't like." That might have been because he had low standards for liking. That might have been because he didn't require much of others. And then one wonders what would have been his reaction if one day he did meet a man whom he just could not like? What I am saying is that the reason for our liking, the reason for our holding back our hand from others in anger, is not just because we see so much good in every other person. Quite frankly, some people just are not very likable. Some people are rather easy to disdain. Some people ask for our anger: the rapist, the robber, the sociopath, the disrespectful, the rude. Nevertheless, the point is that behind the eyes and face of each person we must still see the eyes and face of God. In the breath of each person we must still recognize the breath of God.

❖ ❖ ❖ ❖ ❖

When someone has committed a terrible crime in which lives were lost, many people think that person should be executed. What do you think is behind this call for "capital punishment"? Do you think that capital punishment is a fitting penalty for certain crimes? Are there some people that you hate so much that you wish that they were dead? Do you think that you have to hate somebody in order to think that they deserve the death penalty?

❖ ❖ ❖ ❖ ❖

Therefore, the walls of murder, of hatred, and of contempt, those walls which separate us from others, must either come down or should never be erected in the first place.

Making that a reality is not always easy to do. It especially is not easy to do where there is provocation to do otherwise. Sometimes we feel as if there were good reasons for erecting walls and keeping those walls intact. But when they are there, those walls between us and our neighbors, those walls which cut us off from each other and which make it easy for us to live as if our neighbor no longer lived, we should wrestle with them until they can be pulled down.

There are a number of famous (infamous) walls which were designed to keep people separated from each other. Consider Hadrian's Wall, the Great Wall of China, and the Berlin Wall. Sometimes there are also walls around neighborhoods or around people's property. Do walls ever serve a good purpose? Do you think prisons could exist without walls? Someone once said, "Stone walls do not a prison make." What was meant by that? Read some Robert Frost poems such as "Mending Walls," "After Apple Picking," "The Road Not Taken," "Nothing Gold Can Stay," "Stopping by the Woods on a Snowy Evening," and so forth. In all of these poems he is talking about the human condition, about the human experience of life. Identify with that condition and those experiences. Can you see yourself in them?

❖ ❖ ❖ ❖ ❖

In darkness of mind we sometimes hold on to that old saying which says, "Good fences make good neighbors." We should wonder and ask, "Why? Why is that so? Why must that be so?"

Fences cut life from life, don't they? Fences like hatred. Fences like anger, physical harm, and even killing. They make us dead to one another. There is something that doesn't like a wall.

Our prayer should be that God will help us all to see that we need to eliminate the walls, whatever their nature, that exist between ourselves and our neighbors.

Questions

1. From whom does breath come?

2. What happens when God withholds His breath?

3. Is abortion killing?

4. Is euthanasia killing?

5. Why do we sometimes want to get rid of life?

6. Whose eyes should we see in everybody else's eyes?

7. Who is your neighbor?

8. Hating is like _____.

9. What do "walls" (fences) do to people?

Discussion

1. Violence seems to be very much a part of our way of life. What are some of the ways in which both the entertainment and news media could respond in positive ways to the concerns of the Fifth Commandment?

2. Discuss some of the life/death dilemmas people sometimes have to face.

The Ten Commandments:
The Sixth Commandment

Some people think that religion is old-fashioned, that it is out of date, that it is only for old people. What do you think about all of that? Today we live at a time "after the sexual revolution" (a change that took place in the last half of the twentieth century in the way society thinks about sexual behavior). Therefore, do you think that the Sixth Commandment is old-fashioned and out of date? Remember: your opinions don't count for much unless you can back them up with supporting material — reasons for thinking the way you do.

The Ten Commandments, revealed by God through Moses on Mount Sinai, already over 3,500 years ago, are still as fresh and relevant today as they were back then.

And that certainly can be said about the Sixth Commandment: "You shall not commit adultery."

Martin Luther asks and answers:

What does this mean? We should fear and love God so that we lead a sexually pure and decent life in what we say and do, and husband and wife love and honor each other.

In only two of his explanations to the Ten Commandments does Luther not employ the negative. Eight times in response to the question "What does this mean?" he says, "This means that we should NOT …" (should not do this or should not do that). For example, we should not curse or swear; we should not take our neighbor's property or life or defame his name. But only in the explanation of the First ("You shall have no other Gods") and now of the Sixth ("You shall not commit adultery"), is the negative not used. Only the positive is brought to our attention.

❖ ❖ ❖ ❖ ❖
It often seems as if it is easier to be against something than to be for something. Make a list of things that you are against. Try to make a list of as many things that you are for. Why do you think it is easier to be against something than for something?
❖ ❖ ❖ ❖ ❖

I think that Luther did that intentionally. You see, back in his day in Wittenberg, Germany, it was all too easy to go into a crusade "against" something. Today, too, it is easy to crusade against immoral conduct, for example, or to jump on board condemning this or condemning that. One can usually draw a lot of attention by doing so. Human nature, it appears, is such that one usually can draw as much attention to a subject by storming against it as one can by vigorously promoting it. That applies to baseball as well as to sex.

It is not hard to hook people's prurient interests. Therefore, people seem to perk up as much when you crusade against sex as when you crusade for it. The long and the short of it is that it is usually wise to be careful of folks who are always against most anything and feel that they must censor most everything. There is something perverse about a person who gets his thrills and excitement from bashing things.

❖ ❖ ❖ ❖ ❖
Criticism is often negative, and it hurts to be criticized. Someone once said that for every critical remark we make to someone else we should make twenty positive remarks. Why do you think that is so?

Why do you think that "forbidden fruit" seems to be "tempting"? What are some of the "forbidden fruits" in your life? How do you handle being tempted by "forbidden fruit"?
❖ ❖ ❖ ❖ ❖

Therefore, I think it was for that reason that in his explanation to the Sixth Commandment Martin Luther avoided this all together. Instead of giving us a list of prohibitions ("Don't do this and don't do that") which might only inflame our curiosities and lead to our eventual seduction anyway (forbidden fruit always seems to be more tempting), he decided to place his emphasis on what good things this commandment is inviting us to do. In other words, Luther sidestepped the sensational.

That reminds me of a notation which appeared in a guidebook to an old western ghost town. It stated that the quest for gold, which was not there, caused miners to overlook the rich silver that was there. Sometimes we also miss the treasure because we are looking for the wrong thing. So, instead of being preoccupied with a futile quest for fool's gold, let's look for the silver in the Sixth Commandment, a silver which can contribute so much to the richness of our lives.

The Sixth Commandment says, "You shall not commit adultery." And Luther comments: "We are to fear and love God so that in matters of sex our words and conduct are pure and honorable, and husband and wife love and respect each other."

When it comes to matters of sex, that which is "pure and honorable" is not hard to define. Our consciences do a good job in this regard. Therefore, I would like to focus on the words "love and respect." When one person idolizes another person, when someone says, "I have to have you," he or she is violating who the other person is. The one is removing love and respect from the relationship between two people. You see, a person who says that sort of thing has no real concern for the welfare of that other person. For that person has become nothing more than a "love" object: an object to be used and abused. Sometimes some say, "I just idolize you." When that happens then the person idolized becomes an object, an "it."

It has been said that we should love people and use things. However, it often seems as if we use people and love things. Give some examples of this. These examples might come from your own life experiences or from the experiences of others that have become public knowledge.

❖ ❖ ❖ ❖ ❖

In such circumstances the "I love you" really means "I love me, and you are one of the ways in which I can love me if you let me use you." Obviously, that is very selfish behavior. God never wants another person to be merely regarded as an object. Instead, we are always to look at each other as "loved creatures of the Creator, fashioned by Him in His image." That's what God wants. We are to look at the ones we love as those who carry within them the very breath of God, and even as God is not to be used as an object, neither are persons. The Sixth Commandment warns against using people as objects, especially as sex objects.

Obviously also, the Sixth Commandment speaks against being unfaithful to one's spouse (husband or wife). Included, however, in this unfaithfulness is also a word to those who are able to claim that they have never "'cheated" on their husbands or wives. This is what I mean: Martin Luther said that husband and wife should "love and honor each other." Thus, for example, when a wife becomes merely an accessory to her husband's life to be used for sexual or domestic purposes or as a decoration for his life, then he has violated her person. However, when he loves and honors her, then he is behaving toward her as God behaves toward both her and him. And since we are created in His image, His behavior should be the example for our behavior.

Gomer was a sexually promiscuous woman who very likely had been abused as a child. Was Hosea a fool for taking such a risk in marrying a woman like that? Would you ever take such a risk? Do you think a person like that could ever change his or her behavior?

In our relationship with God, we often are like Gomer. It's not that we are necessarily sexually promiscuous, but we all demonstrate unfaithfulness to God. What does God do about our unfaithfulness? What is the best thing that we have going for us which can possibly help us change our behavior?

❖ ❖ ❖ ❖ ❖

A biblical example of this is the relationship between the prophet Hosea and his wife Gomer. The full account of this can be found in the book of the Old Testament which bears the prophet's name, Hosea. Hosea, a good man, was instructed by God to marry a woman of terrible reputation. Her name was Gomer. The name "Gomer" itself sounds terrible. Who would want to be called "Gomer"? I have never heard of any other woman called by that name. So bad was Gomer's reputation that she has stigmatized that name for all time. Nevertheless, Hosea married Gomer. Perhaps he had high hopes of helping her reform. But Gomer was not about to give up her lovers. She would stay out late at night. She knew all the boys in town, and not only by their first names.

Hosea bewailed his misfortune:

> *It was I who gave her grain and wine and oil. It was I who lavished upon her silver and gold. It was I who took care of her....* (Hosea 2)

But Gomer didn't seem to know that she had it so good. She kept on violating the trust that Hosea had placed in her. Nevertheless, Hosea always took her back. He had plenty of cause to divorce her. He had good reason never to have anything to do with her again. But she was always welcome back home.

Not too many of us have to go through such an extreme ordeal as did Hosea. But the point is this: Hosea was to be a living model, a living example of the goodness and grace that God demonstrates toward His people. God cares for us. He provides for us. He is always ready to take us back no matter how faithless to Him we become.

Throughout the Scriptures we have God presented to us as a faithful God who in spite of our faithlessness does not divorce us. To follow such an example in our relationships with each other, especially in our most important and significant relationship, that which is between husband and wife, that is godliness.

This faithfulness, this fidelity, calls for us to go beyond doing what is merely best for ourselves. It goes beyond doing only that which seems to be of advantage for our own selves. That is because it always flows out of commitment, out of love, for the other person. That love and respect is of the nature of God; that is of the nature of godliness.

❖ ❖ ❖ ❖ ❖
Statistics show that in matters of sex the Christian faith is not a "kill joy." In fact, statistics show that Christians enjoy and appreciate sex more than those who do not accept what the Bible has to say on the subject. Why do you think this is so? Do you think that heterosexual relations within marriage and faithfulness to one's spouse in the matter of sex is biblical? Do you think that it is good? Do you think things would be different in society if people lived their sexual lives according to what the Bible instructs? What might be some of these differences? Do you think that what the Bible says about sexual behavior is subject to various interpretations by various people in various circumstances, or do you think that what the Bible has to say about sexual behavior is objective and constant for all times, all places, and all people?
❖ ❖ ❖ ❖ ❖

In conclusion I would like to share with you a few words about the body. Christians are sometimes judged to be "anti-body," as if the flesh is something intrinsically sinful. Some people actually think that it is. But such a puritanical preoccupation with chastity stifles the spirit. It almost makes us want to despise our flesh.

We must remember, however, that the body is made up of matter, and matter is of God's creating. What makes the human body different from all other created bodies is that the Spirit of God is breathed into it and gives it life. Thus it is that Christians are reminded that their bodies are actually the temples of God, temples in which the Holy Spirit lives.

Also, we should not forget that Jesus, God's Son, did not come to this earth merely as some sort of disembodied spirit. No! He came here as a flesh and blood person. And I am willing to bet that if you had lived at the time of Jesus, and that if you pinched Him, He would have said, "Ouch."

So you can see that the Christian faith is a very real faith. By that I mean that it has to do with the real stuff of life. Therefore, we must be careful about separating the body from the soul. If that is done, then there is nothing left. Consequently, even as we honor the body of Christ (the Christ of flesh and blood) so we also care for our own body and the bodies of others, of all others.

❖ ❖ ❖ ❖ ❖
What do we mean when we say that our sexual behavior is a "matter of faith"?
❖ ❖ ❖ ❖ ❖

It's really a matter of faith you see, of faith in Jesus Christ, God incarnate, God in the flesh. And that matter of faith certainly gives shape and direction to how we live according to the Sixth Commandment.

Questions

1. Why did Luther present his explanation to the Sixth Commandment only in the positive?

2. How are people sometimes treated as sex objects?

3. Who was Hosea's wife?

4. What kind of person was she?

5. What kind of person was he?

6. Why is the example of Hosea so good for us?

7. Why/how is keeping the Sixth Commandment a matter of faith?

8. Why is being "anti-body" unhealthy?

Discussion

1. Violence and sex in the media often seem to be related. Discuss the relationship between the two.

2. What are some things that you think could be done to strengthen a wholesome view of human sexuality?

The Ten Commandments:
The Seventh Commandment

❖ ❖ ❖ ❖ ❖

The First Commandment is number one because of its priority. The Third Commandment is number one because it was the first of all the commandments to be given. The Fourth Commandment is number one as far as human relations are concerned. And the Seventh Commandment is number one as far as being the first to be learned. Can you give a reason for any of the other Commandments being number one?

❖ ❖ ❖ ❖ ❖

"You shall not steal."

The Seventh Commandment has to do with stealing, or perhaps we should say, it has to do with not stealing.

Martin Luther in the *Small Catechism* gives us this explanation of what these words imply:

What does this mean? We should fear and love God so that we do not take our neighbor's money or possessions, or get them in any dishonest way, but help him to improve and protect his possessions and income.

Even though this commandment is number seven in the listing, in some ways we can say that it is number one, because it is the first commandment which we learn. Even if we don't learn it, it is the first commandment which others have tried to teach us. Is it not true that already at the young and tender age of one we all were becoming familiar with this commandment? At that time in life most of us did not have too much trouble yet with skipping church or with using bad language or with hating others or with bearing false witness or with lusting and coveting and the like. But we were already having trouble with putting our hands on things which did not belong to us. Therefore, our fathers and our mothers had to continually remind us, "Keep your hands off." They said that not because they were worried that we would steal a lamp, a vase of flowers, or a television set, but they knew of the trouble that we could get ourselves into if we went about handling everything. As little children we all had to learn that.

Yes, there is a great distance between putting little hands on things they should not be getting on to and out-and-out stealing. Nevertheless, the point is we learn that there are some things for us, and then there are some things for others.

There are some people who think that this division of property which leads to the private possession of property is that which is at the bottom of all the troubles in the world. They say that if we didn't divide everything up as either "mine" or "thine" then there would be no conflict between people. We would then have no fights. We would have no wars. It is, they say, the possession of private property which makes for the great gulf fixed between the "haves" and the "have nots," between the rich and the poor. Therefore, the conclusion is: everything should be shared; that would free our world from tension.

Marxism and the communism of eastern Europe during much of the twentieth century was atheistic. It was based on a philosophical concept called "Dialectical Materialism." However, communism has appeared in many forms throughout the centuries. There was even an attempt at communism within the early church. Refer to Acts 2:44-46 and Acts 4:32-37. Do you think that this form of communism could be successful in our world today? Is using taxes to support welfare a form of communism? Do we find communism on a limited level even within our local congregations? What do you think about a fair and equitable distribution of wealth? Should the world's wealth be divided equally among the earth's people? Do you think some people should have more than others? Do you think some people deserve more than others?

As you think back through the years in history, can you see how economic issues (issues which had to do with wealth and territory) played an important part in wars that were fought?

❖ ❖ ❖ ❖ ❖

That does sound nice — to be able to live in a world free from tensions, to be able to live in a world where we would not have to fear having our homes broken into or in which wars and rumors of war would be no more. And so some, thinking along those lines, have attempted to set up societies in which everything would be held in common, everything would be "common-wealth"; it would all serve the common "weal(th)," and there would be permitted no more private property.

Sir Thomas More, a man of great wisdom and integrity who lived in England at the time of King Henry VIII (and who was executed by that king because he would not compromise his integrity when the king wanted him to — he knew that even if what he was being asked to do was not against the law it was wrong if it was wrong), wrote a book now quite famous titled *Utopia*. ("Utopia" is a Greek word which means a "never-never land," a fantasy land, a "no place." Utopia just does not exist.) In this Utopia everything was held in common, and nobody had more than what was necessary to support his or her life. The Amana Colony in Iowa, the Oneida Colony in New York, and the New Harmony experiment in Indiana are also examples of attempts to set up perfect societies in which private possessions or property and wealth were forbidden. Only the common interest was to be served. But, sad to say, none of those colonies worked according to the original idealism by which they were established. And, according to Sir Thomas More and others, none of them ever will.

❖ ❖ ❖ ❖ ❖

It has been said that "America's business is business." What do you think that means? Is making money the most important thing in the life of an American? Is it the most important thing in your life?

❖ ❖ ❖ ❖ ❖

I think that all of those experiments were unsuccessful because they were all based on the principle that says that holding possessions is evil, that private property corrupts. However, it is not the having of wealth (possessing things in and of themselves) which is evil. Rather, the problem is with the condition of one's heart. It is the attitude of one's heart toward things and wealth which makes the difference. After all, did not Saint Paul write to young Timothy, "The love of money is a root of all kinds of evils" (1 Timothy 6:10)? In the Greek language, the language in which those words were originally written, the phrase "love of money" actually means "to have a passion for silver." Silver was the metal out of which much money was minted then. And the passion for silver often consumed the person within whom it burned.

Coins, which can so easily be held in the hand, are good symbols of that attitude which corrupts the heart. A fistful of coins can easily become one's god. Some will do almost anything to get more of them and to protect those that one has. Doing almost anything ranges all the way from outright stealing to, in the name of "good business," driving a hard bargain at the expense of someone else in the marketplace. Therefore, we are given the commandment, "You shall not steal." Somehow or other God has got to protect us from ourselves.

❖ ❖ ❖ ❖ ❖

Getting more money for an item than what it is worth is sometimes referred to as "driving a good bargain," "making a good deal," or just plain "good" business." Do you think that it is? What might also qualify as "good business"?

❖ ❖ ❖ ❖ ❖

In addition to protecting us from ourselves, the root of this whole problem is basically a mistrust of God's ability to provide for us. You see, greed and avarice come from an attitude which just does not trust God. Greed and avarice betray a lack of faith in God and in His providence. In such a condition we are always worried about being left out in the cold or that somebody is going to get a bigger slice of the pie than we, especially when we are convinced that they have not deserved it but that we have. Therefore, whatever the expense, we grab for more, because we are worried about not having enough.

In the First Article of the Apostles' Creed we confess that God will provide us with all that we need for our daily living. However, sometimes it might seem as if God does not provide. There also are times when it might seem as if we do not have the opportunity to earn honestly what is necessary for our daily support. (For example, a person might be disabled or a company might leave town, and so forth.) Are there ever just causes for stealing? (You might want to refer to Victor Hugo's novel *Les Miserables*.) What are we to do when there just does not seem to be enough daily bread on the table?

❖ ❖ ❖ ❖ ❖

Do you know that Jesus said, "Don't worry," 99 times? Actually we don't know how many times He really said that. But words like that, similar words, have been recorded at least 99 times by the Evangelists. The point is: in His teaching Jesus made very much of instructing those around Him to have faith and trust. "Don't worry," He said. "Consider the birds of the air and the lilies of the field. They neither gather into barns nor own sewing machines, yet the heavenly Father takes care of them. So you think you can do better than He by worrying about it?" And then the conclusion, "Don't be so anxious about tomorrow ... Your heavenly Father knows your needs. Don't you think that He can take care of you?" (Matthew 6 paraphrase)

It is a matter of faith, you see! Therefore, we need not worry about how much we have or about how little we have. Nor do we need to selfishly hoard our possessions — which, by the way, is a form of stealing (a stealing from the world). Nor do we need to feel as if we are in competition with everybody else, seeking advantage over another person by acquiring legally or illegally more and more until we think we are somebody because we have so much.

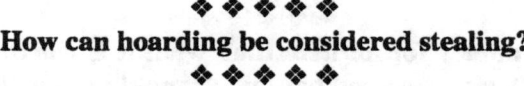

How can hoarding be considered stealing?

❖ ❖ ❖ ❖ ❖

Now let's look at Martin Luther's second half of his explanation to the Seventh Commandment. I am certain that we don't need anybody writing us a book about the evils and criminality of pilfering — stealing the goods that belong to others. There are laws covering that. We simply should not take our neighbor's money or goods. But Luther adds we are to "help him (that is our neighbor) to improve and protect his possessions and income," his means of making a living, his means of providing for his physical needs and the needs of his family.

Is the answer to hunger and the needs of the world's people to be found in this idea of stewardship? What do you think of when you hear that word? Is hoarding, taking the wealth of this world out of circulation, poor stewardship? What would you consider to be good stewardship? Since stewardship has to do with our handling of the world's wealth and that portion which is placed into our hands, what, according to the principles of good stewardship, should be done with the wealth of the world? As a good steward, what responsibilities do you have with respect to the wealth of the world and the needs of its people? Do you think that the answer to the problem of not having enough bread on some tables is to be found in the exercising of good stewardship? What does all of that mean for you as an individual? What does it mean for the Church at large?

❖ ❖ ❖ ❖ ❖

You see, when God talks to us about our relationship to the wealth of the world, it is not a matter of ownership. He owns it all anyway. He is its creator. He is the creator of all the silver and gold which lies beneath the surface of the earth. He is also, we say by faith, the provider of all those things for which we have worked so hard — the silver and the gold which ends up in our hands.

If that, indeed, is the case, that ownership is not the argument, then what is?

It is a matter of stewardship!

Stewardship is recognizing in the wealth of this world blessings from God. These blessings are for our own welfare, and through us these blessings are for the welfare of others. Thus, in the second half of his explanation to the Seventh Commandment, Luther focuses on helping our brothers instead of stealing from them. Yes, we might have the privilege of being a blessing to someone who at this very moment might be standing in need of a blessing from us. In simple words, that means that a good businessman is not someone who looks for opportunity to take advantage of someone, but a good businessman is someone who looks for opportunity to be of service to someone in need. That's a good businessman in God's eyes. He is willing to do what is necessary even if it costs him some of his time, energy, and maybe even some of his money. That is because such a person sees all of what he has as gifts from God's open hand for the welfare of those standing in need. That reminds me of a little riddle: "He who possesses much has little to give. He who possesses little has much to give." That summarizes this concern for stewardship that is included in Luther's explanation to the Seventh Commandment.

❖ ❖ ❖ ❖ ❖
Why do you think Jesus talked so much about stewardship?
❖ ❖ ❖ ❖ ❖

Finally, here is an interesting statistic: Jesus spoke more about stewardship (the handling of wealth) than He spoke about anything else in all four of the Gospels. Now that ought to tell us something about what He considered to be important, to be of value. To Jesus value was not found in things, but value was to be found in how things were handled. So you see, it is a matter of the heart; it is a matter of faith: trusting God that He will provide so that we can share.

Questions

1. Why can the Seventh Commandment be considered in some ways to be the First Commandment?

2. What do some people think is the cause of all the tensions on earth?

3. What was the name of the famous book Sir Thomas More wrote?

4. Give some examples of "utopian" communities which have been attempted but which failed.

5. What is the real problem with possessions?

6. What can a fistful of coins become?

7. How can we steal without really taking anything?

8. What is the real root of the problem with possessions?

9. How many times did Jesus say, "Don't worry"?

10. Hoarding is a form of _____.

11. What are we to do according to the Seventh Commandment?

12. What is a "good businessman"?

13. What did Jesus talk about more than anything else?

14. Quote the quote with which this chapter ends.

Discussion

1. Some say that the next world war will be fought between the "haves" and the "have nots." What is your opinion? If you have one, support it with evidence.

2. White collar crime has become quite a problem in our society. Compare it with violent crime, particularly with respect to violent crime accompanying theft.

The Ten Commandments:
The Eighth Commandment

What is your first name, your middle name, and your last name? Do you know what your names mean? Do you know why you were named the way you were? If you could rename yourself, what would these new names be? The Chinese say that the greatest insult you can give your ancestors is to change your name. Why do you think they feel that way? Some women, when they are married, keep their original last names, or incorporate them into their new names which include the names of their husbands. What do you think about that practice?

Do you know what a person's most precious possession is? Some might want to argue the point, but for the sake of that argument, let me ask again: Do you know what a person's most precious possession is?

My side of the argument says that the answer to that question can be found in the Eighth Commandment: "You shall not give false testimony against your neighbor." I think that the answer to that question is found in the Eighth Commandment because of what Martin Luther says in answer to the question:

> *What does this mean? We should fear and love God so that we do not tell lies about our neighbor, betray him, slander him, or hurt his reputation, but defend him, speak well of him, and explain everything in the kindest way.*

Some people think that a person's most precious possession is (or possessions are) his or her money, wealth, some keepsake, some family heirloom, some trophy or award, or some such thing.

Some people even consider good health to be that which is of most value. "As long as you have your health," they say, "that's the most important thing. Then you are as rich as King Midas."

My argument, however, is that a person's name is that which is of most value.

Now then, what is in a name?

"David" means "One who is loved."

"John" or "Jonathan" means "Gift of God."

"Deborah" means "Bee."

"Eve" means "To live."

Many times new names are assigned by parents to their infant children (even before birth) not because the name well represents some unique characteristic of the child, or even because the name reflects the circumstances surrounding the child's birth, but most likely because the name sounds pleasant to them or the name is popular at that particular time. Much to the chagrin of the child, the name might in time fall out of popularity and consequently be somewhat of an embarrassment to the son or daughter in later years. Sometimes a child is named after some favorite aunt or uncle or some other admired person.

It is even more by chance that we carry our last names. Children have absolutely no choice in the matter, although some later on in life will decide to alter their last names when they get married. I doubt, though, that many brides have turned down a proposal for marriage simply because they did not like the sound of the groom's last name.

I am an "Albertin" simply because years ago the ancestors on my father's side of the family came from that part of Germany ruled by a prince whose name was "Albert." His name was given to that province which he ruled. Therefore, an Albertin is one who belonged to Albert.

If your name is Miller it might be that someone way back on your father's side of the family ran a mill. If your name is Smith it might be that somebody way back on your father's side of the family nailed shoes onto the bottom of horses' feet. And a Johnson is someone who on the father's side of the family was a son of a man named John.

❖ ❖ ❖ ❖ ❖

How do you give value to your name? How does God give value to your name? (Hint: At Baptism you are named and that name gets written into God's Book of Life. What is the Book of Life? Refer to Revelation 3:5.)

❖ ❖ ❖ ❖ ❖

However, as we grow in years our names begin to take on character. We give them character by the way we live.

Let's try a little experiment. Fix in your mind's eye some person of slight acquaintance, someone whom you can picture in your mind, but someone of whose life you do not know many details. Perhaps this person is a new neighbor, or perhaps he or she is a member of your church whom you have seen but with whom you have never really spoken. Now then, what does that person's name mean to you? Probably not much: a name in a phone book; the owner of an address; a shadow who will be remembered no more. The winds of time will blow and he or she will be forgotten.

Not to have a name is to be a "nobody." To be a "nobody" is not to exist. When we can't think of a person's name, that person may not exist for us. How can you get better at remembering the names of people? How important is it for you and for them for you to remember their names? How important is it for you to remember their names in a positive way (rather than in a negative way)?

Nevertheless, that person has been given the gift of life, and that person lives with just as much right to live as do you. That person knows, just as you do, that living is often difficult. He or she has undoubtedly wiped many runny noses and has laughed and cried just as you have. That person has hopes for himself or herself and for his or her children. And then, too, that person enjoys the taste of good food, enjoys good company, and appreciates the moments when left alone. That person has hopes and fears. He feels a lump in his throat and freezes with horror at the thought of cancer. She sees her hair turn grey and knows that someday she will die.

Meanwhile, there are little comforts which, although they mean nothing to you, are much like your little comforts and mean much to that someone whom you have been holding in your mind all the while that you have been reading these words.

Remember! That person has a name! Remember that name!

It represents that person's life! It holds that person's integrity. And right now, at least in your mind, that is all that that person has. For all intents and purposes, you can destroy that person by maligning his or her name.

Both Naboth and Jesus were executed because their names were violated. Can you think of anyone whose life was ruined because of what was said about him or her? The ruining of one's reputation can be next

to fatal, if not fatal. Think of some public person whose reputation was ruined because of what was said about him or her. Were they guilty of what was said about them? Was what was said true? Was it false? If true, do you think the media (radio, television, newspapers, and magazines) have the right and the duty to tell the public about these things? When does the public have a right to know? Are there any times when it would be best to hush and cover up these sorts of things? When it comes to scandal, why do you think that important people get the "front page" while less important people get the "back pages"?

When the "facts" are known about a person, what should we do with those facts?

Two examples from the Bible illustrate this point. One is from the Old Testament, and one is from the New Testament. The Old Testament story was about a man named Naboth. He lived at the time of King Ahab. Naboth had a fine vineyard in the valley of Jezreel, the most fertile area in all of ancient Israel. He was a decent sort of man: honest, hardworking, not pretentious. And he took good care of his vineyard.

Ahab the king, however, admired the vineyard. He coveted it so much that he said to himself, "I must have that vineyard as my very own." So he inquired what was the name of the man who owned it. When he found out that it was Naboth's, he immediately started negotiations to possess it. But Naboth insisted that since it was an ancestral inheritance and carried the name of the family, he would not be able to sell it. That greatly disappointed Ahab. He was used to getting his way. He was spoiled. He pouted.

Jezebel, Ahab's wife the queen, felt sorry for him. She thought that the king should have whatever he wanted. After all, he was the king. So she rigged a trial in which charges were brought against Naboth. Even though what was said was not true, Naboth was accused of cursing both God and the king. False witnesses were brought into the court, and by the end of the matter Naboth was convicted of treason and blasphemy. He was then executed, and Ahab the king, exercising the right of eminent domain, took possession of the vineyard.

The point is this: because Jezebel had false witnesses brought against Naboth, because his good name and character were maligned in court, Naboth, even before he was executed, was as good as dead. They killed him with their words.

"Sticks and stones may break my bones, but words (names) can never hurt me." Is that true?

Consider the power of words to bind up and heal and also their power to hurt and destroy.

❖ ❖ ❖ ❖ ❖

Somewhat parallel to this is this story from the New Testament. I am sure you all know to what I am referring: the trial of Jesus. He, too, was already as good as dead when He was hauled into court and charges were first hurled against him. Lies were leveled against Him by those who wanted to see Him dead. They didn't have any evidence which could convict the man. So it was that in both the court of the land and in the court of the church, they had men "bear false testimony" against Him, saying that "He advocates that taxes not be paid to Caesar ... that, indeed, He wants to be king instead of Caesar ... that He is inciting to riot and revolution ... that He even claims to be the Son of God." True, Jesus did say, "Give to God what is God's," and He did claim to be a king. He did speak of a revolutionary new way of life. He did claim to be God's Son. But whatever He said was twisted and misrepresented, so that the testimony of the witness against Him was used to defame His character. What was said about Him was said in order to injure Him. His accusers wished Him dead. And that's exactly what we do when we "give false testimony" against our neighbor, when we "betray ... slander ... or hurt his reputation."

The other side of the coin is that instead of using our words to injure another person, we should use them (our words) to speak in favor of him or her. Thus Luther commented that when talking of and about anyone else, we should "defend him, speak well of him, and explain everything (about him) in the kindest way." That means that we should always be willing to come to the other person's defense and speak good things about him even if the person is (as we sometimes say) getting what he or she deserves. That's "going to bat" for that person.

If God gave us what we deserved, what would we get? If God called "a spade a spade" what would He say about us? Instead, because of Jesus, what does God say about us? How does God defend us and speak well of us? Why does He do that?

❖ ❖ ❖ ❖ ❖

You see, God will not have anyone deprived of his or her honor or integrity even though there may not be much of a reputation to defend being carried by the person's name in the first place. In addition, even when the laws of the land no longer demand that we do it, and even when those laws are no longer able to do it, we must: we must protect a person's reputation; we must defend his or her name. In fact, that is precisely *when* we must. We must come to the defense of the other person who has been victimized by the words of others. The Eighth Commandment asks us to be the advocate of the person who is the object of scandal.

❖ ❖ ❖ ❖ ❖
Why is it so important for us to come to the defense of someone who has no one to defend him or her? How far are you willing to go in defense of someone? How far was/is God willing to go in your defense?
❖ ❖ ❖ ❖ ❖

That can sometimes be hard to do. For not only do we all enjoy hearing gossip, we enjoy seeing a person put down a peg or two, especially if we are convinced that he or she deserves it. Nevertheless, whatever our motives may be, we are never called upon to sit in judgment over the character of others. Therefore, Luther says that when we hear what we should not hear, our ears should "be like tombs," closed, dead to that kind of information. And as far as our tongues are concerned, they should be equally as mute. We should be dead to that kind of talk, lest with what we now know, with that kind of information, we render someone else as good as dead.

"Sticks and stones may break my bones, but names can never hurt me." We know better than that.

In the name of God, in the name of His Son Jesus the Christ, we have been made whole, healthy, honorable, and of good report. In His name and with His name we are able to be engaged in the task of helping to restore the dignity of the lives of others, remembering that it is in the name of God that we ourselves are restored to the fullness of life. Through the good name of His Son, He gives our tarnished names a new shine, a new sheen.

Questions

1. What is a person's most important possession?

2. What does your name mean?

3. If you could change your name, to what would you change it?

4. What did Naboth have that Ahab wanted?

5. What did Ahab do to get it?

6. What did Jesus' accusers do at His trial?

7. What does it mean when Luther says that we should "put the best construction on every thing"?

8. When we hear gossip, like what should our ears become?

9. Even if what is being said about a person is true, but it is damaging to that person's reputation, what should we do?

Discussion

1. Can you think of someone whose reputation was ruined by gossip? What were some of the details of that situation?

2. On the positive side, discuss how positive reinforcement became prescriptive for someone's life.

The Ten Commandments:
The Ninth and Tenth Commandments

Myths, legends, and fairy tales usually have some historical fact. These stories usually are built on events that happened. The story about the Pied Piper of Hamelin, for example, is based on an incident that actually took place in the Middle Ages in the town of Hamelin. The story of Hansel and Gretel has been repeated many times over in the lives of youngsters who have become lost. Think of some other myths, legends, and fairy tales which have some factual background. Identify these backgrounds.

Aesop's Fables usually use animals but convey instruction for human behavior. Identify a number of fables which have been used to teach morals and values. What are the morals to the stories?

Great literature, the classic novels, does much the same thing. Again, identify both some of these novels and the lessons they teach.

The telling of most fairy tales and myths and legends has long been one of the most effective ways of teaching moral principles and of underscoring lessons of value. Among the more common themes of these stories is the warning against coveting (being greedy) and always wanting more than what you have or need to have. Saint Paul wrote about this to young Timothy:

> *There is great gain in godliness with contentment ... If we have food and clothing, with these we shall be content. But those who desire to be rich fall into temptation, into a snare, into senseless and hurtful desires that plunge men into ruin and destruction. For the love of money is the root of all evils; it is through this craving that some have*

> *wandered away from the faith and pierced their hearts with many pangs.* (1 Timothy 6:6-10)

Speaking about this love of money and fairy tales and myths and legends, I think that the most well known of all such stories is the one we learned when we were in kindergarten. It is the story about King Midas, the man with the golden touch. There are many versions of this story, but the one that I remember best is the one told by Nathaniel Hawthorne. He was an American man of letters, novels, and stories. I remember his version of King Midas so well, because it was at the feet of my kindergarten teacher that I first heard it. Storytelling time was my favorite time in school. I could always picture in my mind just what the teacher was reading or saying.

Here there was old King Midas. Early every morning he would creep down into his vault, the chamber of his palace which held all of his gold. There he would sit and count it — every day, over and over, always wishing that he would have more of it. He had more than anybody else in the whole world already, but he always wanted more.

❖ ❖ ❖ ❖ ❖
It is often characteristic of elderly people to want to hold on to things, and for younger people to grab for things. Why do you think this is so?
❖ ❖ ❖ ❖ ❖

One morning while he was sitting on his stool, running the gold through his fingers, a bright light flashed. It almost blinded him. You see, there was only one small window, high in the ceiling, which let light into that chamber. Every morning, at just the right time, a beam, a shaft of pure golden light, would come streaming through that one little window. On this particular morning, as it came streaming in, it lit on the eyes of King Midas. After he recovered from the shock of the original glare, he saw the figure of a man standing alongside of his gold. The man was golden, sparkling and shining as the purest gold.

King Midas was certain that he had locked the door behind him when he had entered into his private chamber, the vault in which was stored all of his gold. Therefore, he assumed that the man now appearing before him must be no mortal but rather some supernatural messenger from the gods.

The stranger looked around and commented, upon seeing all the gold, that Midas certainly must be a very rich and wealthy man. The king did not deny this, but he was also not long in complaining that, after all, it was not so much considering how long and hard he had worked for every bit of it. The stranger then inquired whether or not the king was happy. Was he satisfied with what he had? Of course, Midas told him that he was not. Well, what do you suppose this stranger said next? He asked the king what would satisfy him, what would make him happy.

Midas saw in this question an excellent opportunity to get what he wanted (all that he wanted), for he was certain that this stranger all dressed in gold could give him whatever he wished (his heart's desire). Therefore, he said that if everything he touched would turn to gold, then he would be the happiest man in the world. (Don't forget Midas had more gold already than what he needed, but all it did was lie around in his vault. Nevertheless, there was still room for more, and he wanted more and more.)

I imagine that you can already see the trouble into which Midas was about to get himself. This is how it happened: he immediately ran out of the vault and into the palace garden which surrounded it. There he reached for a yellow rose, already golden in color. He snatched at it, and immediately it turned into solid gold. He held it to his nose, but its sweet scent was gone. Well, that did not bother Midas at all. He picked a whole armful of such roses and immediately rushed them back to his vault where he threw them onto his mountain of gold, making it even larger. This went on for a while until, quite exhausted, Midas thought he had better stop for breakfast. He called for his servants to bring him something to eat while he sat down in the midst of his garden. At first he was delighted. His fork and his spoon, upon his touch, immediately became pure gold. What a surprise he had when he reached for an orange. It became a ball of pure gold. He could not crack it with his teeth. Then he reached for a goblet of goat's milk. When the goblet touched his lips it became pure gold, and that brought a smile to King Midas' face. However, when the milk touched his lips it too turned to gold. Midas choked as the golden liquid hardened in his mouth. He had no choice but to spit it out — little pebbles of gold.

As he sat there sputtering and coughing golden coins, his dearest daughter approached. Of all that was in the world, next to gold of course, he loved his dear daughter the most. Therefore, as she hurriedly approached her father who was in distress, he reached out his hand for her, but as soon as their fingers touched ... Yes, you know what happened. She became a pillar of pure, lifeless gold.

❖ ❖ ❖ ❖ ❖
Our weaknesses, our sins, often cause difficulty with those things/persons whom we love the most. Why is this so? In your own life, can you recall how what/who you loved the most was hurt by something you did, by your weakness, by your sin?
❖ ❖ ❖ ❖ ❖

It was then that Midas began to see the curse of his golden touch. He wept, and as he embraced his daughter, drops of golden tears fell to the ground.

It was now about noon. The sun was high in the sky. Suddenly its beams streamed around the father and daughter standing there in the garden, the one weeping, the other stone cold. Midas saw in the golden glow the same stranger again standing near. Once more the stranger began to speak; he asked Midas if he was happy now. Was he satisfied now that all that he touched turned to gold?

Of course, Midas then confessed how his greed and avarice for gold had turned into a curse for him, and he begged to be relieved of this curse.

❖ ❖ ❖ ❖ ❖
In order for Midas to be relieved of the cursed Golden Touch, what did he have to do?
❖ ❖ ❖ ❖ ❖

The stranger, not a mere mortal, then gave instructions to King Midas that he should go down to the River Pactolus which flowed nearby and bathe in its water, washing away the curse. He was also instructed to bring back enough water from the river to sprinkle on all that he wanted to be turned back into itself again. Midas, of course, immediately did that.

❖ ❖ ❖ ❖ ❖
Do you see any parallel between Midas washing in the River Pactolus and the Sacrament of Holy Baptism? What does baptism wash away?
❖ ❖ ❖ ❖ ❖

It is said to this day the grains of sand of the River Pactolus carry nuggets of gold which flow from the very spot where Midas bathed. Do you know where the River Pactolus is? For your own good, I am not going to tell you.

That's the story of King Midas and the trouble he got himself into because his heart was greedy for, because he coveted, gold. And it is against the background of that story that what Saint Paul wrote to young Timothy now takes on special meaning. (By the way, both Paul and Timothy knew of the story of King Midas, and they also both knew where the River Pactolus was.)

> *If we have food and clothing, with these we shall be content. But those who desire to be rich fall into temptation, and into a snare, into many senseless and hurtful desires that plunge men into ruin and destruction. For the love of money is the root of all evils; it is through this craving that some have wandered away from the faith and pierced their hearts with many pangs.* (1 Timothy 6:8-10)

❖ ❖ ❖ ❖ ❖
What do you think is the key word in the passage from 1 Timothy 6:6-10? Could it be "content," or "desire," or "love," or "money," or "craving"? Defend your choice.
❖ ❖ ❖ ❖ ❖

That precisely is what the Ninth and Tenth Commandments are all about. "You shall not covet your neighbor's house," and "You shall not covet your neighbor's wife or his manservant or maidservant, his ox or donkey, or anything that belongs to your neighbor."

Again the question is asked in the *Catechism*: "What does this mean?" And again Martin Luther answers the question.

We are to fear and love God so that we do not scheme to get our neighbor's inheritance or house, or get it in a way which only appears right, but help and be of service to him in keeping it.

And,

We should fear and love God so that we do not entice or force away our neighbor's wife, workers, or animals, or turn them against him, but urge them to stay and do their duty.

❖ ❖ ❖ ❖ ❖
Martin Luther's explanations of the Ninth and Tenth Commandments resemble his explanation to the Seventh Commandment. Look for and make the comparisons. Instead of grabbing and hoarding things for ourselves, what should be our primary concern? Do you see how the direction is reflected away from ourselves toward others?
❖ ❖ ❖ ❖ ❖

The implications and applications of these words are many. For example, it seems that we always want more; we seem to always want more than what we already have; it seems that we also often want more than what we need; and sometimes we even want more than what we can handle. In addition, we often also want that which belongs to somebody else. We fight over wills. We fight over property lines. We seem to be more concerned about getting from our neighbor what is his than about helping him keep what is his. In the end that is good for neither him nor us, for you nor for me.

Therefore, when thinking of the Ninth and Tenth Commandments, we do well to remember old King Midas. Remember that the yearning for, coveting, wanting that golden touch is far more of a curse than a blessing.

❖ ❖ ❖ ❖ ❖
How do the Ninth and Tenth Commandments protect us from ourselves?
❖ ❖ ❖ ❖ ❖

I hope that you, too, can now see what is meant by those words that tell us that great godliness comes with contentment.

Questions

1. What is the root of all evil?

2. How much gold did King Midas have?

3. What did he think would make him happier?

4. What was the terrible consequence of his greed?

5. How was he freed from this consequence?

6. What does the story have to do with the Ninth and Tenth Commandments?

Discussion

1. Coveting can sometimes be called "the green eye of jealousy." Reflect on how such jealousy has impacted your life.

2. From literature discuss an example of how coveting destroyed someone's life.

The Ten Commandments:
The Conclusion To The Commandments

What does God say of all these commandments?

He says, "I, the Lord your God, am a jealous God, punishing the children for the sin of the fathers to the third and fourth generation of those who hate Me, but showing love to a thousand generations of those who love Me and keep My commandments."

What does this mean? God threatens to punish all who break these commandments. Therefore, we should fear His wrath and not do anything against them. But He promises grace and every blessing to all who keep these commandments. Therefore, we should also love and trust in Him and gladly do what He commands.

We have come to the end of the Ten Commandments. One by one we have walked through them and have carefully observed what they have said to us.

Set in your mind the following two scenes: 1) Moses delivering the Ten Commandments to the Israelites who were gathered at the foot of Mount Sinai (Exodus 20), and 2) Moses reviewing the Ten Commandments for the Israelites immediately before they crossed the Jordan River to take possession of the Promised Land (Deuteronomy 5). What do you think it must have been like (the day, the location, the crowd of people)? What would have been your response if you had been present? Why do you think that these commandments were given in the first place, and why do you think they were reviewed at precisely this time?
❖ ❖ ❖ ❖ ❖

The Ten Commandments are recorded at two different places in the Bible. The first place is Exodus 20, and the second place is Deuteronomy 5. At both places, immediately following the First Commandment, "You shall have no other gods," and its extension, "You shall not make any graven images," there follows this commentary:

I, the Lord your God, am a jealous God, punishing the children for the sin of the fathers to the third and fourth generation of those who hate Me, but showing love to a thousand generations of those who love Me and keep My commandments.

Although these words especially focus on the First Commandment and our relationship to God as God, Martin Luther saw that these words also apply to all of the Commandments. Therefore, in his *Small Catechism* he put them at the end of the Ten. And that makes sense, doesn't it? For is it not true that how we regard any and all of the Ten Commandments has a lot to say about our relationship to God? It is a matter of faith, you see. Even how we treat one another (Commandments Four through Ten) is a direct reflection of how we respect God. Therefore, these words are a good summary of all.

The Conclusion is divided into two parts. The first part contains a word of warning. In fact, it almost sounds like a threat. "I, the Lord your God, am a jealous God, punishing the children for the sin of the fathers to the third and fourth generation of those who hate Me." In the "What does this mean?" explanation, Martin Luther said, "God threatens to punish all who break these commandments. Therefore, we should fear His wrath and not do anything against them."

God threatens to punish!? Why would He want to do that? Why would He want to do that to His children?

❖ ❖ ❖ ❖ ❖

There is a parenting movement that has gained quite a bit of popularity. It is called "Tough Love." It is based on the principle that if parents really love their children they will make sure that their children realize that there are consequences for unacceptable behavior. Permissiveness is the opposite of tough love. What do you think are some of the positive benefits of tough love? Were your parents tough with you in a loving way? Do you plan to be tough with your children in a loving way? Some think that "tough love" is the hardest part of parenting. Would you agree? What are some of the ways in which the "tough" part can be overdone?

❖ ❖ ❖ ❖ ❖

It is not very easy to warm up to a god who threatens to punish. That especially is true for people like us who live in a rather permissive society. Today it seems as if almost "anything goes." It is hard to tell anybody anymore what one should or should not do. In addition, if God really is so big of heart as we like to say that He is, why worry about hellfire and brimstone anyway? God will understand our behavior, and if it is not what He wants, He will forgive.

That is a dangerous way to think. It can easily lead us into thinking that if there is forgiveness then there are no consequences. I'd like to tell you a story which illustrates, however, that consequences often do continue even after forgiveness has been granted.

This is a story about a man named Achan. You can find his entire story written in Joshua 7. This is what happened: when Joshua led the Children of Israel around the city of Jericho one time each day for six days, and then seven times on the seventh day, the walls of that ancient city fell down. They simply crumbled and collapsed right before the eyes of the Israelites. Joshua had told them, however, that when this would happen, they were not to take any booty or spoils from the city. As you might imagine, it was not hard for the Israelites to defeat the defenders of Jericho after the walls had collapsed. They rushed in and quickly took the city. It was then that the spoils of the war were just too much for Achan to resist. He grabbed some royal robes decked with jewels; he also took 200 shekles of silver and a bar of gold worth about $10,000. He hoped that after they all settled down in their new homes his loot would help him get established in business in his new neighborhood.

Since nobody had seen him take the booty, and so that nobody would see him with it, he hid it all beneath the floor of his tent. But he was not alone in his violation of the law. In order to get all of that wealth out of Jericho, the members of his family most likely helped him do it. Also, they certainly must have been aware of it when he stashed it under their tent. Therefore, they became partners in his crime.

Achan thought that all would be fine. Achan had invested in his future. He was sure that when later on he produced this wealth nobody would associate it with Jericho.

How wrong he was! A few days after the Jericho affair, the Israelites went up against a rather small city called Ai. The Israelites thought that they would have no difficulty in conquering that town. However, they were in for a big surprise! The defenders of Ai prevailed and inflicted some rather unexpected casualties on the Israelites. That immediately signaled to Joshua that God must have had a hand in their defeat in order to call the attention of the Israelites to something that was not quite kosher. As you might expect, an investigation was held, and finally the accusing finger was pointed in the direction of Achan.

Surprisingly enough, Achan did not deny the charges. In fact, he made a full confession of what he had done. And I am sure that he was forgiven — fully forgiven. But this story ends with telling us that Achan and his entire family were executed. That may sound like harsh punishment to us. Indeed, it was and is. But the punishment was to stand as a sign to the rest of the people that there are consequences to be paid for sins committed.

Do you think Achan was treated fairly or unfairly? Do you think that the members of his family should have been included in the consequences of his behavior? What if you had been Achan? What if you

had been a member of his family? How would you then feel about what happened to him (them)? Was what happened to them an example of "tough love" being carried too far?

❖ ❖ ❖ ❖ ❖

Of course there are consequences. Only a fool would say that he can do as he very well pleases without any regard for what might happen — the consequences. An inattentive motorist might even be very sorry for causing an accident, and the persons whom he hit might even forgive him, but there still are two damaged automobiles. A teenager might be very sorry for having binged on beer and her father might even forgive her, but her headache persists. And not only that, but also the consequences of our behavior even affect others. Statistics underscore that many of those arrested and imprisoned for felonies, especially when violence is part of the crime, had fathers who were both alcohol abusers and who physically abused them and their mothers. That is an example of the consequences of sin being passed on from generation to generation. (Without a doubt the behavior of parents does have a significant influence on their children.)

❖ ❖ ❖ ❖ ❖

In addition to consequences for unacceptable behavior (call it punishment), there are other consequences to behavior that is generally not considered good. Identify some of those behaviors and their consequences. What are some of the ways in which society suffers the consequences of the unacceptable behavior of others? Do you think that if people intentionally harm themselves that the rest of society should pay for it? For example, if a person smokes and contracts lung cancer and can not pay for his or her medical expenses, should that person receive Medicaid assistance? What are some other examples of the behavior of some for which society in general suffers/pays the price?

❖ ❖ ❖ ❖ ❖

But dare we call this punishment from God? Can we speak of a God who not only gets angry with us but who also makes us pay the consequences of our behavior?

Of course we can and must. Would God even be God any more if part of His divinity was not a respect for righteousness (rightness)? That question and its answer are much like this question and its answer: could I have claimed to have been a father to my children if I had fostered an "anything goes" policy around our house? Oh, I might claim to have fathered my children, but I hardly could claim that I was a "father" to and for them. Yes, there might have been a lot of protesting around our house when the foot came down heavily. Yes, I might even be accused of being too harsh or unfair at times. In addition, my own anger and wrath probably did at times get in the way of good judgment. But all things considered, I would have done my children an even greater disservice if I had given them the impression that there were no consequences to their actions — whether those actions and consequences were good or bad. There still were and always are consequences.

Even though the above analogy breaks down at some points, for all analogies do sooner or later, nevertheless, the principle is: if God is to be God, then He must be a God of righteousness (rightness); He must be a God of justice. And even though we don't like to blame God for the painful things of this world, and certainly don't accuse Him of initiating suffering, God is a God of judgment. Ultimately that means that not only is His wrath encountered when we violate the rules He has established for the living of our lives, but that also means that there comes the final moment when those whose sins stand, when those whose guilt has not been removed by confession and absolution, when those who have not opened themselves to the gift Christ secured for them on Calvary's cross, will face the consequences of eternal punishment for those sins.

❖ ❖ ❖ ❖ ❖

The Bible contains many examples of God punishing people for their sins. The destruction of Sodom and Gomorrah is one such example (Genesis 19). Name some other examples. Do you think that God still punishes people to this day for their sins? If so, what would you consider to be some examples? Do you think that Hell is too heavy of a punishment? What do you think Hell is like?

❖ ❖ ❖ ❖ ❖

We call God's ultimate judgment "Hell." And there is no real way in which we can soften it up, that is, if we take the Scriptures seriously. Hell is not here on earth. Hell is not just a symbol for the grave. Hell is not even just being away from God, as if that might not be so bad. Hell is hell! It is a terrible "place" in eternity. It is no place that I want to be. It is no place that you want to be. Jesus Himself described it as a place of "weeping and wailing and gnashing of teeth."

The point of all of this is that the Conclusion to the Commandments, and in particular the words of warning and threat found there, say to us that God's justice must be taken seriously if we are going to take seriously the second half of the Conclusion. It is that second half which proclaims that to those who love Him, God is willing to go even further, much further, in His loving and forgiving them. Look, if you will, at this example of divine mathematics: God's righteous wrath might go as far as the third or fourth generation, but His mercy extends to thousands. That's a ratio of at least 250:1, or better yet 333 1/3:1. That is a ratio which is decidedly in our favor.

What do you think about these mathematics of judgment versus forgiveness: 1:250 or 1:333? What does that tell you about God? What does that tell you about what the ministry of God's people (the Church) should be? How much of our energy should be spent in condemning the sins of the world, and how much of our energy should be spent in healing the world?

❖ ❖ ❖ ❖ ❖

I don't know of a better note upon which to end this discussion of the Ten Commandments. Think of it: we might shudder once in a while when we think of God's power and anger directed against sin. But His anger is only a fraction in strength by comparison to the size of His grace and mercy. And it is in that grace and mercy that we place our trust. (It is a matter of faith after all, isn't it?) You see, not only is God's love for us so much greater than His justice, but He is also the very One who gives to us what He expects of us but which we cannot provide for ourselves, namely that forgiveness which provides a peace which surpasses all understanding and which even makes the consequences of sin (as uncomfortable as they might be) pale into the background. Such is the Amazing Grace of God.

❖ ❖ ❖ ❖ ❖

God's justice must be satisfied. Justice demands consequence for sin. How has God ultimately satisfied His justice? (Read Isaiah 53 and Romans 5.)

❖ ❖ ❖ ❖ ❖

With that we now come to the end of our journey through the pages of Dr. Martin Luther's *Small Catechism*. And in our ending we come back to the beginning. Whether as little children or as grown-up adults, we all have a great need of God's love through Jesus the Christ. It is by baptism that we are brought to the faith; it is through Holy Communion that we are kept in the faith. In between we confess the faith; we live with an eye on how God would have us to live; we pray for strength to live that way; we confess our shortcomings when we fail. Always and always we live under God's grace.

As some men of faith used to say, and as many still say, *"SOLI DEO GLORIA."* To God alone be the glory.

❖ ❖ ❖ ❖ ❖

In the matter of Faith and Life why is it appropriate to give God all the credit and glory?

❖ ❖ ❖ ❖ ❖

Questions

1. Where in the Bible are the Ten Commandments recorded?

2. What did Achan do?

3. What happened to Achan and his family even through they confessed?

4. Why (for what purpose) were they punished?

5. What is the ratio between God's love and His punishment?

6. Can you think of a situation in which someone confesses, is forgiven, but still experiences some consequences from what he or she did?

Discussion

1. A distinction can be made between punishment for sins committed and the consequences of sin committed. Discuss the difference between the two.

2. Discuss how the people of God, aware of the consequences of sin, can still minister to those who experience such consequences.